# Guide to
# MARTHA'S VINEYARD

## Praise for previous editions

"Ms. Burroughs writes a definitive guide to this marvelous place that reflects her knowledge of the island in all seasons."

— *Wichendon Courier*

"It is one thing to write a guidebook packed with useful facts and information, but quite another thing to convey a sense of place with intelligence, candor, and style. Polly Burroughs has managed to do both with the graceful flourish that is her hallmark."

—Julie Wells, Editor, *Vineyard Gazette*

"Polly Burroughs combines a vast knowledge of Martha's Vineyard with an insightful and thorough narrative, which together create the ultimate guidebook for visitor and local alike."

—Charlie Utz, Publisher, *Vineyard Style Magazine*

## Help Us Keep This Guide Up to Date

Every effort has been made by the author and editors to make this guide as accurate and useful as possible. However, many things can change after a guide is published—establishments close, phone numbers change, facilities come under new management, and so on.

We would love to hear from you concerning your experiences with this guide and how you feel it could be made better and be kept up to date. While we may not be able to respond to all comments and suggestions, we'll take them to heart and we'll also make certain to share them with the author. Please send your comments and suggestions to the following address:

The Globe Pequot Press
Reader Response/Editorial Department
P.O. Box 480
Guilford, CT 06437

Or you may e-mail us at:

editorial@GlobePequot.com

Thanks for the input, and happy travels!

**INSIDERS'**GUIDE®

# Guide to
# MARTHA'S VINEYARD

Eleventh Edition

**POLLY BURROUGHS**

**WITH PHOTOGRAPHS BY MIKE WALLO**

**INSIDERS'**GUIDE®

GUILFORD, CONNECTICUT
AN IMPRINT OF THE GLOBE PEQUOT PRESS

The prices and rates in this guide were confirmed at press time. We recommend, however, that you call establishments to obtain current information before traveling.

All selections of lodgings and restaurants have been made by the author. *No one can pay or is paid to be in this book.*

To buy books in quantity for corporate use
or incentives, call **(800) 962–0973**
or e-mail **premiums@GlobePequot.com.**

# INSIDERS' GUIDE®

Copyright © 1979, 1981, 1985, 1988, 1990, 1993, 1996, 1999, 2001, 2004, 2007 by Polly Burroughs

All rights reserved. No part of this book may be reproduced or transmitted in any form by any means, electronic or mechanical, including photocopying and recording, or by any information storage and retrieval system, except as may be expressly permitted by the 1976 Copyright Act or by the publisher. Requests for permission should be made in writing to The Globe Pequot Press, P.O. Box 480, Guilford, Connecticut 06437.

Insiders' Guide is a registered trademark of Morris Book Publishing, LLC.

All photographs by Mike Wallo unless otherwise noted.

ISSN 1548-2928
ISBN 978-0-7627-4398-8

Manufactured in the United States of America
Eleventh Edition/First Printing

# CONTENTS

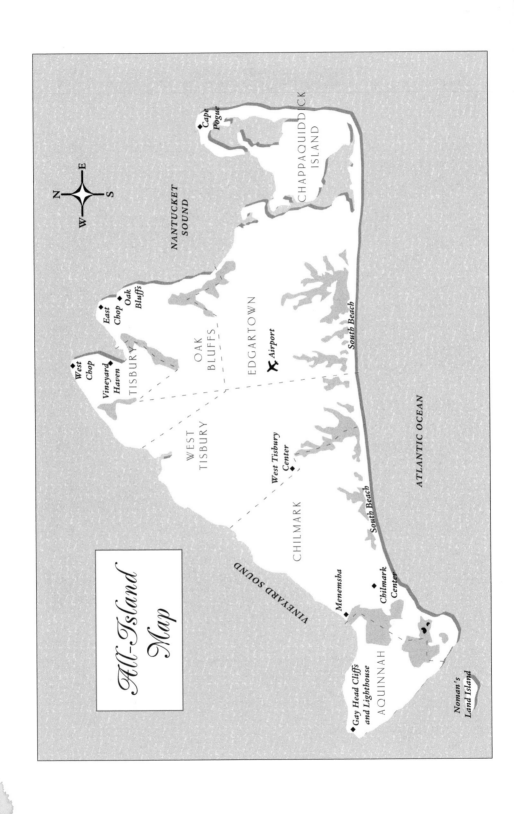

# ACKNOWLEDGMENTS

The author is indebted to the following individuals for their generous assistance in helping to put together this guide: Art Railton, former editor of the magazine of the Martha's Vineyard Museum; Eulalie Regan, librarian at the *Vineyard Gazette,* for her thoughtful assistance; Mike Wallo, production manager of the *Gazette,* for his excellent photography; Ann Nelson, who understands the book world so well; and Lynn Zelem, my editor for this edition, for her helpful suggestions.

# THE ISLAND'S PROFILE

Martha's Vineyard is an island that lies 5 miles off the shoulder of Cape Cod, Massachusetts. Twenty miles long and 9 miles wide at its broadest point, the Island is triangular and encircled by the Vineyard Sound, the Nantucket Sound, and the Atlantic Ocean. With hills, valleys, and flat plains, the Island is as renowned for the beauty of its varied geological landscape as it is for the individual character of its six towns.

A boulder-strewn ridge runs all along the north shore of the Island, extending to the high, rolling moors at the Island's western tip. The wooded, mid-Island outwash plains, which were formed by the waters that flowed from melting glacial ice, reach down to the windswept beaches along the south shore, where fingerlike ponds jut in from the ocean. Estuaries rich with marine and bird life fringe the Island's shores. Four superb harbors are sculpted into the Vineyard and Nantucket Sound side of the Island. From the beginning of time, the sea and winds have shaped and reshaped these contours, just as they have helped shape the Island's human history since the arrival of the first permanent white settlers in 1642.

Of all the Island's assets, the sea and the ocean beaches are the great attraction for vacationers. Once the artery for America's founding and development, and to the Vineyarders their livelihood and only means of communication with the outside world, the sea has once again given the Island its economic base by attracting thousands of vacationers each summer. It is an extremely popular summer resort. The number of hotels, inns, guesthouses, restaurants, and stores, as well as the variety of concerts, lectures, fairs, sports, walking tours, auctions, performing arts, and other activities for the visitor, has increased dramatically since the 1990s. While the winter population of 15,000 has increased slowly through the years, the summer influx of vacationers quickly escalates to about 100,000 seasonal visitors.

To cope with the burgeoning number of visitors each summer, certain changes have been made. There are many more ferries running than in the past; shuttle buses serve all of the towns; free parking arrangements have been made to cope with traffic congestion; and many more places to stay, eat, shop, and rent cars and bikes have become available to the public. And yet not everything has changed, for standards to preserve the scenic beauty of the Island continue as they have for years. There are only a few bathhouses and a couple of food stands at the beaches; there are still no traffic lights on the Island; and signs at many beaches and wildlife sanctuaries warn visitors not to disturb bird-nesting areas, trample or drive on the dunes, or litter.

Despite the growth of the Island population, tradition runs deep in all six of its towns. Evidence of their Yankee heritage is most apparent in the off-season, when the population dwindles. The pace slackens, and Islanders settle down to small-town life with its small-town rhythms.

The six towns are as well known for their individuality as were the early Yankees, whose independent character and idiosyncrasies are legendary. Certain customs have prevailed, and one is the usage of the terms "Up-Island" and "Down-Island," which are important for the newcomer to understand.

When a ship sails in an easterly direction, it is decreasing or running "down" the degrees of longitude toward zero at Greenwich, England. A westbound vessel, on the other hand, is running "up" its longitude. Thus the Down-Island towns are those on the eastern and northeastern ends of the Island: Vineyard Haven, Oak Bluffs, Edgartown, and the island of Chappaquiddick. The Up-Island communities include North and West Tisbury (which are geographically in mid-Island, but considered Up-Island), and Chilmark and Aquinnah, at the westernmost tip. A ship moving through Vineyard Sound sails "up" to New York and "down" east to Maine.

The Island's principal port of entry and bustling commercial center is Vineyard Haven, whose maritime origins are rooted in coastal shipping. The town's residential areas have more year-round homes than are found elsewhere on the Island. There are some attractive and quiet

# Do:

- Pay attention to the posted rules and regulations at all beaches.
- Use bicycle paths if you are bicycling.
- Have the proper light and reflectors when bicycling at night.
- Watch out for one-way streets in the towns. The streets were laid in the nineteenth century, and the narrow ones in the center of all three Down-Island towns are one-way.
- Keep your voice down in the towns during the evening hours. No shouting! This has become a serious problem.
- Be courteous to others.
- Be responsible for your own trash, particularly on the beaches.
- Keep your dog on a leash at all times when in public, and keep your cat confined to your property, out of consideration for others.
- Pay attention to ocean swimming conditions and information about Lyme disease and tularemia.

# Don't:

- Drive on dunes, trample them, or harm the vegetation.
- Pick wildflowers.
- Disturb small clams, scallops, or other shellfish.
- Bicycle on the sidewalks.
- Wear bathing suits in the center of the towns or appear shirtless or barefoot. Rollerblades and bicycles are not allowed in the center of any town.
- Leave litter on any street, beach, or roadway.
- Sleep in your car or on the beach anywhere on the Island. It is illegal.
- Drive over 45 miles per hour; the speed limit is even slower on most roads.
- Dump boat sewage into the harbors. There is a heavy fine.

places to stay a few blocks from the center, and the visitor will find good restaurants, attractive gift shops, and bike, moped, car, and boat rentals readily available. Although the town does have two small beaches, vacationers will probably want to use the big public beaches elsewhere on the Island. Public tennis is available in town, and there's golf in nearby West Chop. Evenings are quiet, but there are many things to do: movies, theater, lectures, and year-round entertainment at the Katherine Cornell Theatre.

The Down-Island town of Oak Bluffs first became popular as a Methodist camp meeting place in the mid-nineteenth century and soon after became a large summer resort, which it still is. It no longer has huge hotels (nearly all were destroyed by fire), except for the Wesley Hotel, but the summer frivolity and seaside boardwalk atmosphere prevail, along with its extraordinary Carpenter Gothic architecture. A merry-go-round, pizza and ice-cream parlors, saltwater-taffy stands, and shops cater to the tourists from the excursion boats running back and forth to the Cape Cod towns of Falmouth and Hyannis, as well as large cruise ships and the Steamship Authority ferries from Woods Hole, which carry cars. The town's U-shaped harbor is jammed with power-boats, and an attractive sandy beach runs along either side of the ferry dock. There are public tennis courts and a golf course. The rates for rooms in Oak Bluffs, which aren't too fancy, are less than those at some other places on the Island.

The visual character of Edgartown evolved from whaling-industry money made during the nineteenth century. With its handsome architecture, brick sidewalks, fences ablaze with roses, and beautiful gardens, it is the prettiest town on the Island. Flags fly everywhere in Edgartown, another reminder of its maritime background. The majority of Edgartown's inns are clustered in the village proper, where there's an endless array of restaurants, gift shops, boutiques, fishing boat charters, the Island's performing arts center, and beaches, all within walking distance. There are public tennis courts and three large public beaches within 3 miles of the center of town and another beach and wildlife reserve on Chappaquiddick Island, a distance of 3 miles from the Island's ferry. The town has become congested in the summertime, so free parking lots outside of town and shuttle bus service have been introduced.

To stay Up-Island, a car is a necessity, as it may be a 5- or 6-mile drive to a beach or a grocery store. With its many sparsely settled areas, it is rural and quiet. West and North Tisbury, which cut across the middle of the Island from shore to shore, have little beach access, and West Tisbury's center seems more like a New England farming community than does any other place on the Island. It has always been a farming community; the annual county fair is here, and there are several riding stables. The Agricultural Hall in the center of town is used for various events, and there are lectures, musical programs, and movies at the Grange Hall. There are a few places to stay, but most visitors rent private homes or beach cottages.

## The Island Idiom

The Island idiom, that wonderful, illogical way of explaining and expressing things, is disappearing. But there are still some around who speak in their unique way and are—inadvertently—very funny.

An old mason had been working on a large fieldstone chimney. One morning, after an hour or so, he just picked up his tools, put them in his truck, and started to leave. "Why are you leaving?" his puzzled employer asked. "Them stones ain't talkin' to me today," he muttered and got in his truck and drove off.

One summer resident ordered a new stove unit to be installed during the winter. She arrived in June for the summer to discover nothing had been done.

"Why didn't you call me?" she asked the appliance man.

"Why should I?" he replied, "They didn't have it."

*The famous Old Whaling Church in Edgartown, built with whaling money, is decorated for Christmas.*

With its high, rolling hills and sweeping views of the Atlantic Ocean and Vineyard Sound, the Up-Island town of Chilmark is beautiful. In recent years its land has become some of the most expensive on the Island. Chilmark has no private clubs, but the Chilmark Community Center is a gathering place for residents and visitors where there are sports—baseball, tennis, but no golf—lectures, concerts, nature walks, and programs for children. Chilmark Center, called Beetlebung Corner, has a summer grocer and a good restaurant, while Chilmark's fishing port of Menemsha has its own beach, several places to eat, a couple of gift and clothing shops, a gas station, a grocer, a post office, and two fish markets. The picturesque harbor is small and crowded with fishing and pleasure boats. There are several places to stay in Chilmark; in addition, private homes can be rented.

The town of Aquinnah on the western tip of the Island is a premier tourist attraction because of the Gay Head Cliffs. The cliffs have a fine restaurant, take-out food stands, and a cluster of tourist gift shops that

## Morning Coffee

While there are many changes taking place on the Island, some traditions remain. Morning coffee is a daily routine for native Islanders and a few retirees, sometimes referred to as wash-ashores. They gather in Edgartown at the Dock Street Coffee Shop, the Woodland Variety and Grill in Vineyard Haven, the Menemsha gas station, where on good days they sit outside on the bench called Squid Row, and the famous Alley's store in West Tisbury. There aren't many secrets in small New England towns, and they gossip, discuss the town news, and voice their political opinions on all matters local and national. These meeting places open early. In fact, to accommodate customers, Conroy's Apothecary in West Tisbury opens at 5:30 A.M.!

*Gay Head Cliffs.*

cater to busloads of sightseers. There are few places to stay in the town other than private home rentals.

Wherever you decide to stay on the Vineyard, you'll find each town has individual character emanating from its historic roots. The scope of things to do and the variety of places to go in each town have fascinated and delighted visitors since the nineteenth century.

# 2

# A BRIEF HISTORY

There have been many theories and much speculation about early explorers landing on Nantucket, Martha's Vineyard, and Cape Cod, but the first written observations about the Vineyard were made by the Reverend John Brereton and Gabriel Archer, who sailed from England to these shores in 1602 aboard Captain Bartholomew Gosnold's ship. According to their reports and the authoritative research by two prominent English historians, David and Allison Quinn (published by the Hakluyt Society in London in 1983), they made their first landfall on Cape Pogue on Chappaquiddick. The Quinns noted that "the probability that it is Gosnold's first [sighting of] Martha's Vineyard is very high indeed."

They went ashore, and Brereton noted in his report: "Going around about it, we found it to be foure English miles in compasse without house or inhabitant." Both men were impressed by the vegetation and berries; the strawberries were "bigger than ours in England," and bushes— raspberries, blueberries, huckleberries, and grapevines—were familiar. Brereton continued, "Such an incredible store of vines, as well in the woodie part of the Island where they run vpon every tree, as on the outward parts, that we could not goe for treading vpon them." They were equally impressed with the ducks, geese, and other wildfowl, the beach peas growing on the sandy shore, and "huge bones and ribbes of whale." Archer wrote of similar impressions but also stated, "We named it Martha's Vineyard," which historians believe was for Gosnold's daughter Martha and possibly for his mother-in-law, Martha Golding. The Vineyard part of the name came from the masses of grapevines they saw everywhere.

The vessel moved on to the main island, where they encountered Native Americans (they had only seen evidence of inhabitants on Chappaquiddick). Brereton wrote: "Yet we found no townes, nor many of their houses, although we saw manie Indians, which are tall, big boned men, all naked, sauing they couer their priuy parts with a blacke tewed skin, much like a Black-smiths apron, tied about their middle and betweene their legs behinde: they gaue vs their fish readie boiled, (which they carried in a basket made of twigges)," and shared their tobacco, which they smoked in pipes made of hard, dry clay. The Native American name for the island was Noepe, meaning "amid the waters."

These Native Americans were of the Pokanocket Confederacy, who inhabited the surrounding islands as well. Also called Wampanoags, meaning "Easterners," they belonged to the Algonquian linguistic group, which extended in a great semicircle from the Carolinas up into Canada and west to the Rocky Mountains. At the time the Pilgrims landed, Massasoit was the sachem, or chief, of the Algonquian Confederation.

FROM THE AUTHOR'S COLLECTION

*Looking toward the waterfront in Edgartown circa 1896.*

FROM THE AUTHOR'S COLLECTION

*A paddle-wheel steamer at the pier in Vineyard Haven Harbor circa 1900.*

Gosnold weighed anchor and sailed up Vineyard Sound to Cuttyhunk Island, the outermost in the Elizabeth Island chain that stretches out from Woods Hole. They stayed most of the summer here and loaded their vessel with sassafras root, skins, and furs bartered from the friendly Native Americans before they returned to England.

Forty years later, in 1641, Thomas Mayhew of Watertown, Massachusetts, purchased for 40 pounds the Vineyard, Nantucket, and the Elizabeth Islands from two English noblemen who held conflicting grants to the area. The following year his son, Thomas Mayhew Jr., arrived with a group and chose Edgartown for the Island's first white settlement. They called it Great Harbor. The town's official name was bestowed by Governor Lovelace of New York in 1671 (when Martha's Vineyard was for a time part of New York) in honor of Edgar, infant son

*The paddle-wheel steamer* Martha's Vineyard *leaves Oak Bluffs while vacationers wave from catboats used for an afternoon sail.*

*A party from Edgartown at a daylong outing to Gay Head Cliffs, June 13, 1918.*

of the Duke of York, heir apparent to the British crown. Both Dutchess County and Queens County in New York were named at the same time. The town subsequently became the county seat for the Vineyard and the Elizabeth Islands.

These first settlers found the Native Americans to be a handsome, disciplined, and peaceful tribe, as Brereton had noted. The Native Americans' economy was based on fishing and farming, rather than hunting, and they willingly shared their knowledge of taming the wilderness, whaling alongshore, gathering fruit and shellfish, seining the creeks for herring in the spring, catching cod and eel in the winter, hunting wild game, and planting corn in the spring. Thomas Mayhew began his work to Christianize the Native Americans, and the little settlement grew slowly. (There were about eighty-five white people on the Island in 1660.) Fifteen years later, his son was the first of many Islanders to perish at sea. Thomas Mayhew Jr. had left Boston on a mission to England, and his vessel was never heard from again.

His father continued to Christianize the Native Americans, as did three succeeding generations, earning themselves the name "Missionary Mayhews." They exercised an important influence over the Island's growth and character. There was never open hostility between these settlers and the Native Americans, although Governor Mayhew's authority as chief magistrate was eventually challenged by other settlers, who accused the Mayhews of running a feudal state. As time passed, Native Americans were edged off the richer lands on the Island; the white settlers did, however, purchase these lands, not confiscate them. Some Native Americans moved off the Island to the mainland, and others moved to Chappaquiddick or to Aquinnah, which is now one of the two Native American townships in the state.

By tradition, these early English settlers were farmers, and gradually settlements other than Edgartown took root on the Island. They became almost totally self-sufficient fishing and farming communities where boats and fishing gear were used equally with plows, wagons, and harrows. Not only were pigs, chickens, and cows in the barnyard, but great flocks of sheep roamed the moors. There were mills along the north

*Zeb Tilton aboard the* Alice Wentworth *with his grandson and crew (far left).*

# Zeb Tilton

There were many famous seamen in the Vineyard's long maritime history. The most unforgettable character was Captain Zebulon Northrop Tilton, the Paul Bunyan of the coast-wise schooner trade, who became a legend in his time.

Zeb was known in every port from South Street to Maine, where he moved freight under canvas for half a century. Born in 1867, he was a huge, skilled seaman, and it was said he could sail to Chicago in a heavy dew. His celebrated life afloat and ashore, and his love of women and colorful wit, attracted a gathering wherever he put into port. He said he knew the coast so well that he could tell where he was when the fog was as thick as cotton batting by tasting the water! Walter Cronkite referred to Zeb and his schooner as "a salty, funny story of a ship and her master."

The stories about Zeb and his extraordinary career live on—and though he was too plain a figure for fancy words, the late Henry Hough, owner of the *Vineyard Gazette*, called him a "stronger and braver Cyrano, a wittier and leaner Falstaff."

Zeb's story is detailed in the book *Zeb*, published by The Globe Pequot Press, and a documentary film is scheduled for release in the spring of 2008.

shore to grind corn and make brick and paint from clay. Vineyarders wove their own cloth from the sheep's wool, evaporated the seawater for salt, hunted wild game, grew their own vegetables, and fashioned their farm tools on anvils.

From the earliest times, Vineyarders also looked to the sea and maritime trade for their livelihood. They exported cranberries, wool, candles, whale oil, and salt cod, which, with New England rum, were the basis of Yankee trade with the Catholic countries of Europe as well as the Azores, the Cape Verde Islands, and the West Indies. The growth of Vineyard Haven was directly proportionate to the expansion of maritime trade between the American colonies and the West Indies, as the town became a primary anchorage for vessels moving up and down the coast.

Whaling became Edgartown's principal industry. Although sheep farming on the Island was successful, it was the sea, with its possibilities for adventure and profit, that lured man and boy down to the waterfront. For more than two centuries, the majority of Vineyard men earned their living as fishermen, merchant seamen, whalers, or pilots, sailing aboard barks, packets, coast-wise schooners, sloops, and even clipper ships.

## Early Immigrants

African Americans and other immigrants of color have had a place in the social structure of the Island since the early nineteenth century. The maritime industry brought people to the Island from Africa, the Cape Verde Islands, Asia, the West Indies, and Europe. Many who had signed aboard ship in foreign countries chose to stay on the Island. William Martin, an African who was an able seaman, became captain of his whaling ship and lived with his family on Chappaquiddick. Some immigrants became domestics as well as farmers. Others migrated to the Island from the West Indies, signing aboard schooners moving freight under canvas. As time went on and Oak Bluffs became a homogeneous summer resort, the immigrants became influential in all facets of the business, art, and religious communities of the Island.

*A farmer in Gay Head circa 1928.*

Edgartown and Vineyard Haven reached the peak of their prosperity in the nineteenth century. By 1914 the completion of the Cape Cod Canal and the increased movement of freight by steamship, train, and truck, rather than under sail, signaled the decline of Vineyard Haven's busy port. In addition, the discovery of petroleum in 1859 had undercut the whaling industry, whose end was hastened by the loss of Yankee ships during the Civil War; by World War I the industry was finished.

Changes came slowly, but they were irreversible. Oak Bluffs came into being as a popular Methodist camp meeting place in 1835, and eventually it became the Island's first summer resort. The resort business became increasingly important through the years and has now replaced everything else to become the Island's primary source of income. Despite all the changes, the towns have continued to retain their individual characters: Edgartown with its handsome whaling captains' houses and stately elms; the summer holiday frivolity of Oak Bluffs with its gin-gerbread architecture; Vineyard Haven, the Island's commercial center; the farming community of West Tisbury, whose agricultural origins are still strong and seem far from the sea; the meeting of sea and soil in Chilmark, where gray, weathered farmhouses dot the rolling moors; Gay Head, now called Aquinnah and still a Native American township; and Menemsha, which is the last true fishing village on the Island.

In many ways the Island still retains a rural lifestyle. There are over thirty farms producing fruits, vegetables, flowers, beef, lamb, and poul-try. Vacationers attend the weekly farmers' market, where they can pur-chase this fresh produce as well as jams and jellies made with the local cranberries, beach plums, other fruit, and rose hips. But in recent years large mansions have been built around the Island, and many residents feel it is destroying the character of the Vineyard.

# 3

# WHEN TO GO

Martha's Vineyard has four distinct seasons for the visitor to consider, and, of course, summer is the most popular. The weather is pleasant; with the prevailing southwest winds, the air temperature averages seventy degrees. On clear, brilliant days the sky is a radiant blue and the sea is a collage of vivid blues and greens. The Island's many beaches are crowded with people tanning, playing in the sand, or swimming in the gentle waters of the sound or the rolling surf along the south shore. The warm Gulf Stream offshore and the surrounding sandy shoals, which the sun warms more easily than deep water, cause the water temperature to range from the sixties to the low seventies.

At other times a smoky southwester blows all day, or a fog rolls in from offshore, cloaking the harbors and beaches in muffled stillness. A mournful moan of a foghorn drones, and most boating traffic stays in port. On these days the towns are jammed as crowds flock in to shop, eat, or visit the museums and art galleries.

All summer long there is a wide variety of entertainment nightly, and the typical summer resort activities are available during the day. There's also a constant flow of special events during July and August—house tours, auctions, art shows, parades, celebrations, festivals, fireworks, sailing regattas, road races, lectures, and a county fair.

This very busy high season slows down on Labor Day with an enormous exodus of visitors. Many people still come to the Island through the early fall, but nowhere does it seem crowded. The wonderful weather lingers for weeks because of the surrounding sound and ocean, which are slow to cool off. During those lovely September and October days, when the water is still warm enough for hardy swimmers, a yellow haze hangs over the moors in the mornings, the middays are filled with a false warmth, and the evenings are cool. The still autumn nights are beautiful; the towns are quiet, and a harvest moon casts its glow across the still harbors, silhouetting the few ships riding at anchor.

Out on the beaches at this time of year, the beach plums have turned a succulent purple, the marsh grasses fringing the tidal ponds and the highbush blueberry turn a palette of fall colors, and purple asters and goldenrod blanket the fields Up-Island. The Beetlebung trees turn a brilliant red at Beetlebung Corner. The seaweed also has shed its summer growth. The shallow waters are crystal clear, and the slanting sun sparkles on the water like crumpled tinfoil. The ponds are filled with migrating birds stopping to rest and feed. Summer residents are closing up their houses and cottages all through the fall. Shipyard workers are hauling and storing boats everywhere. Scallopers are busy launching their small workboats before October, when they start dragging for the succulent bivalve that is such an important part of the winter economy.

For the visitor at this halcyon time of year, most of the shops and restaurants are open, although some have limited hours. One big fall attraction is the Fishing Derby from mid-September to mid-October. Tivoli Day in Oak Bluffs includes bicycle races and a street fair as well as several handcraft fairs, an international-film festival, and the Windsurfing Regatta on State Beach. In addition to these major scheduled events, there are many things for the visitor to do (see chapter 10, Annual Special Events). There are nature walks, bird walks, sports from golf and tennis to horseback riding on the beach, movies, and occasional lectures and concerts. Picnicking on the beach at this time of year, tucked behind a dune if the wind comes up, can be delightful.

By late fall fewer restaurants and shops are open, but those that are gear up for the popular Thanksgiving weekend. The inns are full, ferries are sold out on certain dates, private homes are reopened, and shops are brimming with Christmas gifts for visitors.

By now the Up-Island towns are sparsely populated, while the Down-Island towns, which relate much more closely to the mainland, begin to prepare for the Christmas holiday. All through the fall many residents, young and old, have been working at various handcrafts and making jams and jellies in preparation for the Christmas season. By mid-December the handsome, white whaling captains' houses and beautiful churches are decorated with the traditional holly and greens. Edgartown's Main Street is lined with small Christmas trees running

*A typical harborfront scene with boats lying at anchor in Edgartown Harbor.*

down to the waterfront where the fishing fleet comes in from offshore for the holiday. The second weekend in December, Edgartown has a special "Christmas in Edgartown" celebration. Many shops are closed for the winter, but there are walking tours of the historic houses, some stores and restaurants remain open, carols ring out from the St. Andrew's Episcopal Church belfry, horse-drawn carriages ride around town, Christmas concerts are held at the Old Whaling Church, and there's a parade. Vineyard Haven has its "Twelve Days of Christmas," with Santa arriving on the ferry. The stores and sidewalks are decorated in Christmas greens, there are horse-and-buggy rides around town and holiday performances at the Katherine Cornell Theatre, and most stores and restaurants stay open all winter.

Winter on the Vineyard is very quiet, and the weather is usually moderate, with an average temperature of thirty degrees. Snow lasts only a few days, but the dampness can be penetrating. Bone-chilling raw winds sweep across the empty beaches, and nor'easters—sometimes as severe as hurricanes—batter the Island and delay the ferries. Occasionally the harbors freeze over.

Even so, the winter population has increased in recent years. Retired people as well as young men and women do handcrafts, art, carpentry, boatbuilding, and other occupations through this quiet season. There are winter activities for these residents and any visitors: a mid-Island ice-skating rink, several health spas, an amateur theater group, indoor tennis, indoor pools at the high school and the Mansion House Hotel in Vineyard Haven, special programs at the Old Whaling Church, the Katherine Cornell Theatre, and a selection of lectures and courses at the Nathan Mayhew Seminars. Cross-country skiing on the beach and dunes is a special treat for as long as the snow lasts. Evening entertainment at the Seasons, Offshore Ale, and Lola's in Oak Bluffs goes on all winter and periodically in other bars and bistros.

The ocean is slow to warm up, so spring comes slowly to the Island; but as the days get longer and warmer, the pace begins to quicken. The cool, crisp May days, when the sky seems a particularly brilliant blue and white gulls soar overhead, are truly beautiful. The banging of hammers, the smell of paint—those white houses have to be painted all the time due to the dampness—the launching of boats, and the repairing of lobster pots by fishermen in Menemsha are certain harbingers of another season approaching. Shops and restaurants once again clean, paint, and decorate to prepare for summer, which officially begins in mid-June. Actually, most places open on Memorial Day weekend or a bit earlier. As the days go by, houses and cottages are opened and gardens are planted. The shipyards accelerate their work schedules to a frenzied pace as they rush to paint, repair, and launch boats, and ferry reservations become harder to obtain without advance planning.

The visitor at this time of year will find the days crisp and cool, so swimming is out, but a picnic on the beach out of the cool wind coming off the water can be very pleasant. An early-spring drive or bike ride around the Island is a joy, as the shadbush is in bloom—one of the first signs of spring—with showery, white flowers cascading from its branches. The chirp of pinkletinks (the local name for spring peepers) can be heard from the ponds; along the roadways and sandy shores, white beach-plum blossoms burst into bloom. With the trees still bare and the beaches still empty, the Island's outlines stand out vividly at this time of year, particularly when you view them from the Up-Island hills. From there it looks as though the Island has withdrawn a little while longer before being temporarily "loaned out" to visitors for another season.

In whichever season you choose to come, you'll find this island unique and interesting.

# 4

# HOW TO GET THERE

You can reach Martha's Vineyard by air, by ferry, or in your own boat. Choosing which form of transportation to take will require some planning; your choice will be determined by how much time you have to spend in getting to the Island and whether you will want your own car on the Island or prefer to leave your car in New Bedford (and fly or ferry) or in Falmouth (and take a ferry).

## Car

The most commonly used transportation to the Island are the ferries and cruise boats, which sail from four different towns and are easily reached by car. One ferry port is New Bedford, an hour's drive south of Cape Cod on the Massachusetts coast, and another is Quonset Point, Rhode Island. Two others are Woods Hole, which is at the beginning, or shoulder, of Cape Cod, and Falmouth, adjacent to Woods Hole. Ferries also originate in Hyannis, which is midway along the south shore of the Cape (locally referred to as the mid-Cape area).

To get to the Cape, it might be helpful for you to know the mileage from key cities.

**Washington, D.C. — Woods Hole** . . . . . . . . . . . . .478 miles
**New York — Woods Hole** . . . . . . . . . . . . . . . .271 miles
**Hartford, Conn. — Woods Hole** . . . . . . . . . . . . .187 miles
**Providence, R.I. — Woods Hole** . . . . . . . . . . . . .85 miles
**Boston — Woods Hole** . . . . . . . . . . . . . . . . . . . .85 miles

It is about 20 miles from the Cape Cod Canal to Hyannis or Falmouth and a bit farther to Woods Hole.

With the summer traffic, it can take you longer to reach the Cape than at other times of the year, so be sure to allow yourself extra driving time. It might take an hour to drive from the Cape Cod Canal to Hyannis in summer traffic.

Driving from New York City to Woods Hole may take six hours. Take Interstate 95 to Providence, Rhode Island; from there take I-195 east to Cape Cod. There are numerous signs to the Cape and Islands. At the Bourne Bridge, which spans the Cape Cod Canal, follow the signs to Falmouth and Woods Hole. As you enter Falmouth, you'll see a large Steamship Authority parking lot for those who want to leave their cars on the mainland. There is a shuttle bus service from this parking lot down to the ferry at Woods Hole.

The drive from Boston to Woods Hole takes about two hours in moderate traffic, but it can take much longer in heavy summer traffic. From downtown Boston take the Southeast Expressway (Route 3), turn right just before the Sagamore Bridge (which also spans the Cape Cod Canal), follow the canal for 3 miles to the Bourne Bridge, and follow the signs to Falmouth. If you're going to Hyannis, take the Sagamore Bridge over the Cape Cod Canal and continue on the mid-Cape highway (Route 6) to Route 132, which leads down to Hyannis.

If you're coming from the south or west and plan to leave your car on the mainland, you'll save an hour or more in driving time by taking the New Bedford ferry, which is for passengers only. Take exit 15 in New Bedford and head south toward the waterfront. Follow the Vineyard ferry signs to Leonard's Wharf. The parking lot is a distance from the ferry wharf, so allow yourself plenty of time.

# Bus

Bonanza Bus Lines provides frequent bus service from Boston's South Station and Logan Airport to Woods Hole, stopping in Bourne and Falmouth en route.

Bonanza Bus service is also provided to Hyannis and Woods Hole from the New York City Port Authority Terminal (with a stopover in Providence, Rhode Island). The service is daily and year-round (888–751–8800). Bonanza meets most Woods Hole ferries, providing direct service to South Station and Logan Airport. There are also private limousine services from the Woods Hole and Hyannis ferry docks to Boston, Logan Airport, or other cities you request.

# Cruise Ships and Ferries

If you leave your car on the mainland when you visit the Vineyard, you have more choices as to which cruise ship to take. These ships originate in three places: New Bedford, which avoids all the Cape Cod congestion and summer traffic; Woods Hole or Falmouth at the beginning of the Cape (or what is locally known as the upper Cape); and Hyannis, which is midway along the south shore of the Cape. Hyannis may be a good choice if you are staying on the Cape and visiting the Vineyard.

# Private Boat

If you'd like to sail to the Island in your own boat, there are four harbors offering dockage facilities. Menemsha, at the western end of the Island, has a small, attractive harbor with slips that provide electricity. For details, call the harbormaster at (508) 645–2846. Vineyard Haven has moorings, dockage with plug-ins, launch service, and marina services. The harbormaster can be reached at (508) 696–4249. Oak Bluffs has a tightly packed, U-shaped harbor. Motorboat or sailboat slips with plug-ins

# FERRY INFORMATION

**NOTE:** Prices for all ferry trips are subject to change. Please visit Web sites listed for times.

**The Steamship Authority:** (508) 477-8600 or (508) 693-9130; www.steamshipauthority.com.

### Woods Hole to Martha's Vineyard*

One-way car fares:

    January 1 to March 31 $38.00

    April 1 to October 31 $63.00

One-way passenger fares:

    Adults $6.50

    Children 5-12 $3.50

    Children under 5 free

    Bicycles an additional $3.00 one-way

*The only ferry that carries cars

**The *Island Queen:*** (508) 548-4800; www.islandqueen.com.

### Falmouth Harbor to Oak Bluffs

May to October, passengers only:

    Adults $15.00 round-trip

    Children 12 and under $7.00 round-trip

    Children 2 and under free

    Bicycles $6.00 extra

**Hy-Line Cruises:** (508) 778-2600 or (800) 492-8082; www.hy-linecruises.com.

### Hyannis to Oak Bluffs

*High-speed Ferry* (55 minutes)

April to November, passengers only:

    Adults $59.00 round-trip

    Children 5-12 $42.50 round-trip

    Bicycles $12.00 extra round-trip

*Traditional Ferry (2 hours, 15 minutes)*
May to October, passengers only:
    Adults $37.00 round-trip
    Children 5-12 $19.00 round-trip
    Bicycles $12.00 extra round-trip

**Oak Bluffs to Nantucket**
*High-speed Ferry between Islands*
June to September, passengers only:
    Adults $27.50 one-way
    Children 5-12 $16.00 one-way
    Bicycles $6.00 extra one-way

**The *Pied Piper*, (508) 548-9400; www.falmouthferry.com.**
**Falmouth to Edgartown***
May to October, passengers only (1 hour):
    Adults $30.00 round-trip
    Children 5-12 $24.00 round-trip
    Children under 5 free
    Bicycles $8.00 extra (round-trip)
*Reservations required on weekends

**New England Fast Ferry Co., (866) 683-3779;**
**www.nefastferry.com.**
**New Bedford, Mass. to Martha's Vineyard Express**
January to October, passengers only (1 hour):
    Adults $58.00 round-trip
    Children 3-12 (traveling alone) $30.00 round-trip
    Children under 13 with parent free
    Bicycles $10.00 extra (round-trip)

Continued

**Vineyard Fast Ferry, (401) 295-4040;**
**www.vineyardfastferry.com.**

### Quonset Point, R.I. to Oak Bluffs

May to October, passengers only (90 minutes):

Adults $69.00 round-trip

Children 4-12 $46.00 round-trip

Children under 4 free

Seniors 60 or older $64.00 round-trip

Bicycles $10.00 extra (round-trip)

*The Hy-Line's catamaran,* Lady Martha, *operates seasonally from Hyannis to Oak Bluffs.*

*Boats at anchor in Edgartown Harbor.*

and marina services are available (508–693–9644), and there are some moorings out in the harbor. (It is very crowded in midsummer.) The Edgartown harbormaster (508–627–4746) rents moorings. They have no plug-in facilities, which has helped to keep the waterfront from becoming too cluttered. Moorings out in the harbor are available for rent by the day, week, or season. The shipyard provides marina services.

There are now pump-out facilities for boats in Edgartown Harbor. After extensive studies, Edgartown has initiated innovative regulations to keep the harbor clean, and they are strictly enforced.

# Plane

Air traffic in and out of Martha's Vineyard has increased dramatically in recent years. Cape Air (508–771–6944; www.flycapeair.com) is the busiest airline in the area. The airline carriers serving the Island constantly vary, but there is always year-round service from the New York area, Boston, New Bedford, Hyannis, Providence, and Nantucket. There may also be seasonal service from Westchester County in New York and Bridgeport or Hartford in Connecticut. It is best to check with your travel agent or the Martha's Vineyard Chamber of Commerce (508–693–0085) to find out which airlines are currently operating. Parking at the Martha's Vineyard Airport is $10 per day. The airport is very busy, and in August 2006 there were over 9,000 arrivals and departures, from 737s to single-engine prop planes.

Taxis meet all regularly scheduled flights at the Martha's Vineyard Airport, where there also are several car-rental agencies.

Private planes have access to the Martha's Vineyard Airport, but in the height of the summer season, there may be so much congestion that you should call ahead to make sure there is adequate space for your plane. Call (508) 693–7022 or visit www.mvyairport.com. Private planes also land at the small airport in Edgartown, where the landing field is a grass strip.

# 5

# HOW TO GET AROUND

If you arrive on the Vineyard without your own form of transportation, you will be pleased to find taxis and buses available, as well as car, bicycle, and moped rentals.

## Taxi

Taxis meet all the ferries and scheduled plane flights. Taxi fare is about $15 from Vineyard Haven to Oak Bluffs and about $25 from Vineyard Haven to Edgartown. All fees are subject to change, so call first to confirm rates.

Some year-round taxi companies serving the Down-Island towns are:

**Marlene's Taxi, Vineyard Haven,** (508) 693–0037
**Atlantic Cab, Oak Bluffs,** (877) 477–8294
**All Island Taxi, Oak Bluffs,** (508) 693–2929 or (800) 540–3705
**Stagecoach Taxi, Edgartown,** (508) 627–4566
**Bluefish Taxi, Martha's Vineyard Airport,** (508) 627–7373
**Jon's Taxi, Edgartown,** (508) 627–4677

Limousine service is available on the Island and in Woods Hole. Check the phone book or the chamber of commerce.

## Bus

There is now islandwide bus service, and the Up-Island schedule from late June through early September includes Chilmark, West Tisbury, Aquinnah, and the airport. Shuttle bus service between the three Down-Island towns runs in the off-season as well. In the summer season the buses run twice an hour, and off-season they run hourly. The bus stops are next to the ferry ticket office in Vineyard Haven, behind the police station beside Ocean Park in Oak Bluffs, and on Church Street across from the Old Whaling Church in Edgartown.

Edgartown provides seasonal bus service from the outside of town into the center of town. You may park your car on the edge of Edgartown in the parking lot behind the post office, which is at the juncture of the inland road to Vineyard Haven and the road to Oak Bluffs. You may also park in the school parking lot just off upper Main Street. Parking is free. The buses run every fifteen minutes to downtown. It is advisable to use the bus system, as parking in Edgartown and traffic congestion have become big problems in the summertime. The Martha's Vineyard Regional Transit Authority has been expanding its routes and schedules. Currently, there are eleven routes in operation around the Island, with limited service off-season and extended service from June 24 through September 4.

There are also tour buses in Vineyard Haven and Oak Bluffs that meet the ferries and offer tours that go all around the Island, as well as service to the airport and Aquinnah. Advance reservations are not necessary. The trip around the Island takes about two hours, and those buses that go out to Gay Head Cliffs stay long enough for passengers to get a quick lunch at one of the take-out places there. Taxi vans also meet the ferries at Vineyard Haven. Passengers can share the van, if they wish, for a sightseeing tour. There is continuous daily shuttle service in Vineyard Haven between the ferries and a town parking lot off State Road.

# Bicycle, Moped, and Car Rental

These rentals are available in the three Down-Island towns. The majority are in Vineyard Haven, clustered near the ferry dock, while those in Oak Bluffs are, for the most part, right at the beginning of Circuit Avenue and the adjacent harbor area. Edgartown has a couple of bicycle-rental places and a car-rental office but no moped rentals.

*A whaleboat at the Edgartown town dock, with the Old Sculpin Art Gallery in the background.*

# Island Idiosyncrasies

For newcomers, the Island idiom—those colloquial phrases that are generic to Island life—may sound strange. "On-Island from off" describes a visitor; "off from on" a resident. A favorite adjective among the old-timers is "some"; some good, some bad, some lucky, etc. Up-Island and Down-Island may confuse the newcomer, too. Down-Island describes the towns on the eastern end of the Island: Oak Bluffs, Edgartown, and Vineyard Haven. Up-Island, which is the western end of the Island, includes West Tisbury (which is really in the center of the Island) and North Tisbury, Chilmark, and Gay Head (which changed its name to Aquinnah, the Wampanoag Indian name) at the western tip.

Severe stormy weather always brings familiar queries among the townspeople in the stores, the post office, and other gathering spots: "Are the boats running?" or "Did you get stuck on the other side?"

If you take time to understand the Island and its people a little bit, you'll find it well mannered, charming, quirky, and a little different here. And to the Islanders, visitors come in all stripes and behavior—summer people, summer not.

Listings of all types of vehicles can be found in both the Yellow Pages of the local phone book and the newspapers. Car-rental agencies include Hertz, Atlantic, Budget, AAA Island Auto Rental, and Consumer Car and Truck Rental.

To rent a car during the busiest times in midsummer or on big holiday weekends, it's best to reserve ahead of time. Ask the hotel or inn where you're staying for assistance, or check with your local travel agent.

# Bicycling

Bicycling on the Island is a great deal of fun because the Vineyard has varied terrain. It will be helpful for you to know the distances and terrain if you're thinking about bicycling around the Island. Look for the bike paths in many areas.

### From Vineyard Haven to:

Oak Bluffs (via shore route), *flat, one hill* . . . . . . . . . . . . . . . . 3.4 miles

Edgartown (via shore route), *flat, one hill* . . . . . . . . . . . . . . . . . 9 miles

Edgartown (on the inland road), *hilly* . . . . . . . . . . . . . . . . . . . . . 8 miles

West Tisbury, *partly hilly* . . . . . . . . . . . . . . . . . . . . . . . . . . . . . 7 miles

Chilmark Center, *hilly* . . . . . . . . . . . . . . . . . . . . . . . . . . . . . . 12 miles

Aquinnah, *very hilly* . . . . . . . . . . . . . . . . . . . . . . . . . . . . . . . 19 miles

The airport, *partly hilly* . . . . . . . . . . . . . . . . . . . . . . . . . . . . . . 5 miles

### From Oak Bluffs to:

Edgartown (via shore route), *flat* . . . . . . . . . . . . . . . . . . . . . . . 5.5 miles

South Beach at Katama, *flat* . . . . . . . . . . . . . . . . . . . . . . . . . . 9 miles

Aquinnah, *hilly* . . . . . . . . . . . . . . . . . . . . . . . . . . . . . . . . . . 20 miles

Chilmark (via Airport Road), *partly hilly* . . . . . . . . . . . . . . . . . 16 miles

### From Edgartown to:

South Beach at Katama, *flat* . . . . . . . . . . . . . . . . . . . . . . . . . . . 3 miles

West Tisbury, *hilly* . . . . . . . . . . . . . . . . . . . . . . . . . . . . . . . . 8.5 miles

The airport, *hilly* . . . . . . . . . . . . . . . . . . . . . . . . . . . . . . . . . 4.5 miles

Cape Pogue and Wasque Beach on Chappy, *one hill* . . . . . . . . . . 3 miles

### From West Tisbury to:

Chilmark Center, *hilly* . . . . . . . . . . . . . . . . . . . . . . . . . . . . . . 5.4 miles

Aquinnah, *very hilly* . . . . . . . . . . . . . . . . . . . . . . . . . . . . . . 10.5 miles

### From Chilmark Center to:

Aquinnah, *very hilly* . . . . . . . . . . . . . . . . . . . . . . . . . . . . . . . . 6 miles

Menemsha, *one hill* . . . . . . . . . . . . . . . . . . . . . . . . . . . . . . . . . .2 miles
Menemsha to North Tisbury (via the
    North Road), *hilly* . . . . . . . . . . . . . . . . . . . . . . . . . . . . . . . .6.5 miles

**From North Tisbury to:**
Vineyard Haven (via the State Road), *one hill* . . . . . . . . . . . . . .6.5 miles
The Lambert's Cove Road, a loop off State Road, *hilly* . . . . . . . .4.5 miles

Special bike paths run between Oak Bluffs and Edgartown alongshore and on the inland road between Vineyard Haven and Edgartown; from Edgartown to West Tisbury; Barnes Road from the airport to the inland Vineyard Haven–Edgartown Road near the high school; from the intersection of Vineyard Haven–Edgartown Road and County Road to Oak Bluffs; and from Edgartown out to South Beach. More are being planned, so watch for them. A small ferry takes your bike across Menemsha Harbor to the flat Lobsterville Road. This avoids the steep hills from Chilmark Center to Aquinnah.

Locking up your bicycle while you do errands or go sightseeing in the three Down-Island towns is necessary because of the enormous number of bike riders on the Island. The towns now have bike racks; watch for them. Bikes and mopeds aren't allowed in town centers.

# Bicycle Safety

1. Ride on the right-hand side of the road with the traffic and
   in single file. Use bike paths whenever possible.
2. A headlight and rear reflector are required.
3. Hand signals are required in Massachusetts:
     left hand raised for a right turn
     left hand extended straight to the left for a left turn
     left hand extended and held low for slowing or stopping
4. Children under thirteen years old must wear helmets.

Bicycle rentals are available in Vineyard Haven, Oak Bluffs,
and Edgartown.

# 6

# WHERE TO STAY

Your choice of a place to stay on the Vineyard will depend on the type of holiday you prefer. Every sort of lodging is available, including inns, hotels, motels, rental houses, efficiency apartments, cottages, campgrounds, and a hostel (though you will not find all of these in every town). A complete list of accommodations is available from the chamber of commerce. The hotel listings in this chapter are my own recommendations.

With few exceptions, the Island's inns resemble bed-and-breakfast places in other areas. Some are very elegant, while others are simple. Most provide a continental breakfast, and some serve a full breakfast. A few places with dining rooms that are open for lunch and dinner also serve the general public.

Most of the historic inns are furnished with antiques and have limited outdoor space, so they are not appropriate for small children. The efficiency apartments or larger hotels with separate cottages that have open grounds and a pool or beach are much more relaxing for a family.

Some places are open on a seasonal basis, from early spring to the middle of autumn; others are open year-round. The rates vary according to the seasons. The general rule is that summer (in season) is from June to mid-September. Spring and fall rates encompass April, May, and mid-September to mid-November, also known as the shoulder season. Winter rates at year-round places are the least costly. In-season prices can range from $125 per night for a double room to $600 and up for a suite in the finest places.

If you're planning a week's stay, apartments, cottages, or two-room suites with kitchenettes are convenient and economical. Prices for these efficiency units range from $500 to $2,500 per week, depending on location, size, and number of occupants. Off-season rates are at least 30 percent less; it's best to inquire about them.

Private homes are available through various real estate offices in the towns. Most are listed with the chamber of commerce. Rates run from several thousand dollars per month to $100,000 for the largest waterfront homes for half a season. On-site inspection is always the best idea for any long-term rentals.

If you are planning a summer visit to the Island, the earlier you make your reservation the better; January is not too soon. If you wait until spring, you may not be able to obtain your first choice in the hotels or inns, some of which have cottages and suites that are always in demand.

In this guide the general in-season price range per night for two is as follows: expensive, $250 and up; moderate, $150 to $249; and inexpensive, up to $150. Be sure to inquire about discounts and provisions for children.

# Edgartown

There are many inns, hotels, shops, and restaurants within easy walking distance of this town. Three large public beaches are within 2 or 3 miles. Edgartown is especially popular in the summer months, so be sure to make a reservation as early as possible. The following is a selection of some of the charming places to stay.

## Inns

### The Charlotte Inn
*27 South Summer Street*
*(508) 627–4751*
*Open year-round. Expensive.*

There are several nineteenth-century houses in this inn complex, which has beautifully landscaped grounds and attractively appointed guest rooms that lend elegance and charm to the whole compound. The rooms are furnished with French and English antiques or reproductions. A complimentary continental breakfast is included, and a full breakfast is available. The inn's excellent restaurant, the Terrace, serves lunch and dinner to the general public and has limited dinner hours in the winter. Not recommended for children under fourteen.

### The Shiverick Inn

*5 Pease Point Way*

*(508) 627–3797*

*www.shiverickinn.com*

*Open year-round. Bed-and-breakfast. Expensive.*

Built in 1840 during the height of the whaling era by the town's leading physician, this is one of Edgartown's most elegant inns. Although it was originally a foursquare Greek Revival house, additions and changes were made through the years, many by the original owner's widow, who was impressed by the grandeur of Southern mansions. The large front hall with high ceilings and sweeping staircase is a striking introduction to the sophisticated blending of handsome American, French, and English antiques and Oriental rugs in the drawing room. The adjoining plant-filled garden breakfast room, where a full breakfast and afternoon tea are served, is charming.

On the second floor there are eleven large rooms with private baths and working fireplaces, a two-room suite, and a little outside deck for all the guests to use. Decorated with period-piece wallpapers, the attractive rooms are furnished with antiques and canopied beds. The inn is smoke-free and just a few steps from the center of town.

### The Victorian Inn

*24 South Water Street*

*(508) 627–4784*

*www.thevic.com*

*Open year-round. Moderate to expensive.*

The charming fourteen-room Victorian Inn has matching period-piece furniture, both antiques and reproductions, to create a delightful ambience. It is listed in the National Register of Historic Places, which might well have pleased Captain Lafayette Rowley, the original owner. There are twin, double, queen-, or king-size beds and some canopy beds. Many rooms have harbor views and balconies where smoking is permitted.

A complimentary full breakfast, as well as tea in the afternoon, is served in the dining room or out on the terrace. There are no TVs or phones in the rooms.

### The Edgartown Inn
*59 North Water Street*
*(508) 627–4794*
*www.edgartowninn.com*
*Seasonal. Bed-and-breakfast. Inexpensive to moderate.*

Profits from a successful whaling voyage around the Horn to the Pacific in 1798 enabled Captain Thomas Worth to build this home. His son, William Jenkins Worth, was successful in a different career when he became a hero in the Mexican-American War and gave Fort Worth, Texas, its name. Through the years many prominent people have stayed at the inn, including Daniel Webster and Nathaniel Hawthorne.

The main building has air-conditioning and private baths. A delicious country breakfast is available in the restaurant or out on the terrace.

Across the courtyard are the Barn, with five rooms, and the Garden House, with three rooms, two of which have private balconies. Each room is furnished in white wicker and decorated with delightful, summery, Laura Ashley–style curtains, wallpaper, and bedding. Both buildings have private and semiprivate baths.

### Ashley Inn
*129 Main Street*
*(508) 627–9655, (800) 477–9655*
*www.ashleyinn.net*
*Open year-round. Moderate.*

This delightful whaling captain's house has a large living room with a fireplace, separate dining room for a full breakfast, and a large backyard— a rarity in Edgartown.

The ten bright, cheerful rooms all have TV, phones, and private baths, and there are two large, lovely suites on the third floor with a cot available. Tea by the fire is served on cool days. Nonsmoking. Children ten and older only.

### The Lightkeepers Inn
*25 Simpson's Lane*
*P.O. Box 488*
*(800) 946–3400*
*Fax (508) 627–4611*
*www.thelightkeepersinn.com*
*Open year-round. Moderate to expensive.*

Tucked away on a side street a block from the harbor and the town's center, this charming historic house, home of Edgartown's lighthouse keeper years ago, has been converted into five attractive suites; there's also one cottage.

Each suite has a little kitchen and dining area, a bathroom, and an attractive sitting room with a sofa bed. The two-bedroom suite is ideal for families, and the cottage in the back has a completely private terrace. They permit one-night lodging, which is most unusual.

### The Colonial Inn
*38 North Water Street*
*(508) 627–4711, (800) 627–4701*
*www.colonialinnmvy.com*
*Seasonal. Moderate to expensive.*

In addition to twenty-eight attractively furnished rooms, many with views of the harbor and town, there are six one- and two-bedroom luxury apartments called the Residence Club. These tastefully decorated apartments, with porches overlooking the waterfront, are for sale on a fractional-ownership basis. These fractionals provide deeded ownership of a room for at least four weeks of usage per year. Fractional ownership of second/summer homes is becoming a popular option in many upscale inns.

All guests of the inn may use the spa as well as the fitness room. There are a few retail shops on the first floor, plus Chesca's Restaurant.

### Hob Knob Inn
*128 Main Street*
*(508) 627–9510, (800) 696–2723*
*www.hobknob.com*
*Open year-round. Moderate to expensive.*

This is a charming spot, with sixteen spacious rooms furnished with a mix of antiques and comfortable pieces. A delicious full breakfast is available on the terrace or in the dining room, and afternoon tea is also served. Bicycles are available for rent as well as the inn's 27-foot Boston Whaler for fishing and sightseeing. They also have a conference room, exercise room, sauna, and massage room and will provide a picnic lunch.

### The Arbor Inn
*222 Upper Main Street*
*(508) 627-8137*
*www.arborinn.net*
*Seasonal. Moderate to expensive.*

The nine rooms with private baths here are nicely decorated with a mixture of antiques and contemporary furniture. They all have TVs and air-conditioning, and they serve a continental breakfast. The inn is on Upper Main Street several blocks from the center of the village. There are several umbrella tables out on the back lawn, and there's an antiques shop on the property.

# Hotels

### *Harborside Inn*
*3 South Water Street*
*(508) 627–4321, (800) 627–4009*
*www.theharborsideinn.com*
*Seasonal. Inexpensive to expensive.*

A step off Main Street are three large whaling captains' houses with the names of the original owners over the doorways. Inside and beyond, the buildings have been radically changed and enlarged. With two newer buildings on either side, the Harborside Inn is now a large, U-shaped, time-sharing resort complex around a swimming pool and boat piers that extend out into the harbor. There are eighty-nine rooms and suites, and the gardens are lovely. Many rooms have balconies looking out on the harbor, and all have TVs, air-conditioning, phones, Internet access, and refrigerators. There's also a community room with a stove, and piers are available for those with a boat. Meals are not included in the room cost. The hotel is suitable for children, and there are wheelchair-accessible rooms and suites on the ground floor. The inn arranges all owner rentals if necessary.

### *Clarion Martha's Vineyard*
*227 Upper Main Street*
*(508) 627–5161, (800) 922–3009*
*www.clarionmv.com*
*Open year-round. Moderate.*

This contemporary, thirty-four-room hotel is tastefully decorated in reproduction antiques. The rooms are cheerful and large with modern baths, air-conditioning, color television (satellite system), radio, and, telephone. The hotel serves a continental breakfast. Conference rooms and a hair salon are on the premises. The individually climate-controlled rooms make it comfortable in the off-season. Wheelchair-accessible rooms are available. There is ample parking in the rear. The Grill on Main, a restaurant next door, is excellent.

### Winnetu Oceanside Resort

*South Beach*

*(508) 310-1733*

*www.winnetu.com*

*Seasonal. Moderate to expensive.*

This is a wonderful, beautifully thought-out addition to the Island's hotel scene. With magnificent ocean views everywhere, the site has a long history. It was a Victorian hotel, a naval base during World War II, and a deteriorating condominium complex, and is now a completely rebuilt inn with forty-eight studios and suites, all with porches.

The amenities are extraordinary: For those who leave their car on the mainland, there's a ferry from Falmouth Harbor to Edgartown, where another small boat takes you up-harbor to Katama. Once there, bike, taxi, and bus transportation is available. The immaculate rooms all have attractive kitchenettes. You'll find tennis instruction, a heated pool, babysitting and special children's programs, groceries from town delivered to your door, a general store nearby, a library, elevators, and lovely hallways decorated with seashore murals. There is a fine restaurant on the second floor, facing the ocean. This is a real winner.

### The Harborview Hotel

*131 North Water Street*

*(508) 627-7000*

*www.harbor-view.com*

*Open year-round. Expensive.* .

This grande dame of Vineyard hotels, whose original 1891 building is now restored, is a beloved Island landmark. The 127 bright, cheery rooms, including the modern addition in the rear, have private baths, telephones, air-conditioning, television, and Internet access. The apartments and white clapboard town houses in this twelve-acre complex have fully equipped kitchens, and they are ideal for children.

The front veranda of the original building is furnished with period-piece old-fashioned rocking chairs, where guests may enjoy a sweeping view

*Old-fashioned rocking chairs on the porch of the Harborview Hotel face the Edgartown Lighthouse.*

across the pond to the handsome Edgartown Lighthouse, which marks the entrance to Edgartown Harbor. Sailboats and yachts move through the outer harbor, and Chappaquiddick Island is in the distance. There's a large heated pool surrounded by lush gardens in the back, and a swimming beach by the lighthouse in the front. Tennis and golf are available. Wheelchair accessible. They serve breakfast, lunch, and dinner. This gracious jewel has been an Island favorite for more than a century.

### The Kelley House

*23 Kelley Street*
*(508) 627–7900*
*www.kelley-house.com*
*Seasonal. Expensive.*

The main building was an eighteenth-century inn, but there are now several more buildings, which comprise sixty rooms in all, some with kitchen units. While the colonial decor is charming, such modern conveniences as a television, air-conditioning, and a telephone in each room are welcome, and there's a complimentary continental breakfast. There's also a swimming pool, and laundry services are provided. Wheelchair-accessible rooms are available. Located in the center of town, it's adjacent to, but not on, the harbor. The inn's pub, with the original eighteenth-century rough-hewn beams and ballast brick walls, is delightful, as is the light fare served from 11:00 A.M. to 11:00 P.M. daily.

## Apartments

### Fligor Apartments

*69 North Summer Street*
*(508) 627–4722*
*www.fligors.com*
*Seasonal. Expensive.*

Trim, neat, and very quiet, but only 2 blocks from the center of town, these four attractive housekeeping cottage apartments are a real find in Edgartown. Bright and cheery, they have contemporary furnishings and telephones, TV, air-conditioning, and heat. There's also one two-bedroom house.

### Edgartown Commons

*Pease Point Way*
*(508) 627–4671*
*www.edgartowncommons.com*
*Seasonal. Inexpensive to moderate.*

Two blocks from the center of town is a complex of thirty-five efficiency apartments, motel rooms, and a playground area with swings, sandbox, and slides. A small, fenced-in pool and shuffleboard are on the grounds. All the units have kitchens and television. The largest of the units, simply furnished in a conventional manner, can accommodate six people; it has two bedrooms and a sofa bed in the living room. There is ample parking. Some apartments are in the large, old main building, which was originally the North School. The small lane running between the back of this building and the pool area is Mill Street, once the site of one of the town's gristmills.

# Oak Bluffs

In the summertime, with all the crowds on Circuit Avenue and along the waterfront, Oak Bluffs really rocks. There's a merry-go-round, a noisy amusement center full of slot machines, live entertainment in many restaurants and along the harbor, saltwater taffy, a seafood festival, street fairs, a "monster shark tournament," and speakers and musical programs at the Tabernacle. Passengers from the large cruise ships offshore wander the streets shopping and admiring the rainbow-colored gingerbread houses, as do the regular summer visitors.

There are many bed-and-breakfast places in Oak Bluffs, but only one large, old-fashioned hotel and one attractive motel a half mile from town. Many vacationers live on their powerboats or rent one of the little gingerbread-trimmed houses or the much larger Carpenter Gothic houses.

Lined primarily with powerboats along the U-shaped harbor, the dock's boardwalk is a cluster of gift shops, five restaurants, and a car-rental office. It is also the port for the seasonal *Island Queen* ferry from Falmouth and the Hyannis Hy-Line boats, including the Hy-Line's seasonal catamaran, *Lady Martha.* (The dock for the large Woods Hole ferries, which run from spring to fall, is outside the harbor.)

### Island Inn

*Beach Road (P.O. Box 1585)*
*(508) 693–2002*
*www.islandinn.com*
*Open year-round. Inexpensive to moderate.*

This sprawling motel complex is set in a grove of oak and pine trees overlooking a golf course and Nantucket Sound. Each of the fifty-one units has a kitchen, fireplace, private bath, television, telephone, and air-conditioning, and they are much more tastefully decorated than the average motel room. One two-story building in the complex has high ceilings with bleached timbers and post-and-beam construction. Some rooms have a circular staircase to a loft bedroom with bath. The older suites are a bit larger than other rooms. The cabins facing the golf course have their own porches. Convenient for families with children, the complex has tennis courts, a swimming pool, and Lola's, a good restaurant serving breakfast and dinner, located next door. Wheelchair accessible.

### The Oak House

*Seaview and Pequot Avenues (P.O. Box 299)*
*(508) 693–4187, (800) 245–5979*
*www.vineyardinns.com*
*Seasonal. Bed-and-breakfast. Inexpensive to moderate.*

A few blocks from the center of Oak Bluffs, on the shore road to Edgartown, is this large Victorian home, the summer residence of Massachusetts governor Claflin in the 1870s. The house has dark-stained oak paneling everywhere and period-piece wicker and Victorian furniture. Guests can enjoy the sunroom and the spacious living room with its piano. The handsome exterior has a large, open veranda enclosed by a magnificently carved railing and pastel-painted, fancy shingles. The ten guest rooms, all with private baths, are bright and sunny. Many look out on Nantucket Sound, which is just across the road. A continental breakfast and afternoon tea are served. Children older than ten are welcome. Open May to October.

### Beach House

*Seaview Avenue*
*(508) 693-3955*
*www.beachhousemv.com*
*Open year-round. Inexpensive.*

Queen-size brass beds, wicker, a bit of Victorian furniture—nothing fancy—and the beach right across the street make this an inviting, typically Oak Bluffs inn. There's TV in each room, and a complimentary breakfast is served.

### Narragansett House

*46 Narragansett Avenue*
*(508) 693-3627, (888) 693-3627 (reservations only)*
*www.narragansetthouse.com*
*Open year-round. Inexpensive to moderate.*

White wicker, stained-glass windows, reproduction Tiffany lamps, rainbow-colored woodwork everywhere—this is Oak Bluffs circa 1880, and it's delightful. The thirteen rooms are small and full of character, with modern conveniences like air-conditioning, private baths, and Wi-Fi access. They serve a continental breakfast.

Iroquois Cottage, the purple house across the street, part of Narragansett House, has six rooms and is equally charming with a few more modern conveniences such as cable TV and telephones, a sitting room with Victorian sofas, and other period-piece decor.

### Capricorn House

*79 Seaview Avenue*
*(508) 693-2848*
*www.capricornhouse.com*
*Seasonal. Inexpensive to moderate.*

The beach and the sea are just across the street from this 1876 Victorian house. The seven rooms all have private baths, and there are little porches off some of the rooms that provide expansive views across

Nantucket Sound. The rooms are very plain, with some antiques, and the location is wonderful. Continental breakfast is served.

### The Wesley Hotel
*70 Lake Avenue (P.O. Box 1207)*
*(508) 693–6611*
*www.wesleyhotel.com*
*Seasonal. Bed-and-breakfast. Inexpensive to moderate.*

Near the center of town, facing Oak Bluffs Harbor, is this four-story, gingerbread-trimmed hotel remaining from the turn of the twentieth century, when Oak Bluffs was in its heyday. At that time there were several huge hotels in town, but they were eventually destroyed by fire.

The striking exterior, with its rococo, Carpenter Gothic trim, has a long veranda facing busy Oak Bluffs Harbor, which is just across the street. The foyer has retained its antique decor, including an old-fashioned registration desk, heavy, dark-stained oak trim, and old photographs on the wall; an attractive cocktail lounge has been added. The first floor has some wheelchair-accessible bedrooms that are especially convenient. A continental breakfast is served. Children are welcome.

The front rooms look out to the harbor, which is filled with powerboats and the ferries that run back and forth to Cape Cod.

### The Dockside Inn
*Circuit Avenue Extension*
*(508) 693–2966, (800) 245–5979*
*www.vineyardinns.com/dockside.html*
*Seasonal. Moderate to expensive.*

This is a charming spot only a step away from the harbor and all its hurly-burly, and it's amazingly quiet. Victorian inside and out, the twenty-two rooms include several suites with spacious kitchens and all modern amenities. They are attractively decorated in bright summer colors with Victorian lamps and furnishings and a little porch area for each room. All the rooms have private baths, queen-size beds, air-conditioning, cable TV, and telephones. Some rooms are wheelchair accessible. A recreation room in the back is handy for children, and there's a lovely terrace where you can take your continental breakfast. Open April to October.

### Admiral Benbow Inn
*81 New York Avenue*
*(508) 693–6825*
*www.admiral-benbow-inn.com*
*Open year-round. Inexpensive to moderate.*

Located a short walk from the center of Oak Bluffs, this turn-of-the-twentieth-century inn with its mixture of period-piece furnishings is in a delightful, quiet spot. All rooms have private baths and are nonsmoking. They serve a nice continental breakfast in the dining room or out on the flower-filled terrace. Children are welcome.

### Surfside Motel
*7 Oak Bluffs Avenue*
*(800) 537–3007*
*Fax (508) 693–7343*
*www.mvsurfside.com*
*Open year-round. Inexpensive.*

Right in the center of Oak Bluffs, these very spare motel rooms are convenient and allow dogs. Each room has a private bath, air-conditioning, cable TV, private phone, broadband Internet access, and refrigerators.

# Vineyard Haven

Vineyard Haven, the Island's business center, has a few places to stay within easy walking distance of the town. It has many shops and some good restaurants, but because it is a dry town (which may change soon), it is much quieter in the evening than Oak Bluffs and Edgartown. It has one small town beach near the ferry wharf, extending to Owen Park, and boat, bike, car, moped, and sailboard rentals are easily available along the waterfront. The town has a large residential area heading out toward the West Chop Lighthouse, where there are many house rentals. You may bring your own alcoholic beverages.

### The Thorncroft Inn
*460 Main Street (P.O. Box 1022)*
*(508) 693–3333, (800) 332–1236*
*www.thorncroft.com*
*Open year-round. Moderate to expensive.*

In a delightfully quiet woodland setting a mile from town, this rambling structure and several smaller buildings on the property are well known for their special appointments and services: large, tastefully decorated rooms with canopied beds; wood-burning fireplaces; central air-conditioning; Jacuzzis or hot tubs in some rooms; cable TV and VCRs in all rooms; a full complimentary breakfast; and the *Boston Globe* at your door each morning.

Afternoon tea is served to guests, and the inn is entirely nonsmoking. Bring your own alcoholic beverages. Their many awards are well deserved, including the AAA Four Diamond Award, which they have received every year since 1990.

### 60 Mount Aldworth
### The Doctor's House Bed and Breakfast
*(508) 696–0859*
*www.doctorshouse.com*
*Open year-round. Moderate to expensive.*

In a quiet residential area on the east side of Vineyard Haven, this attractive inn is surrounded by a spacious lawn and attractive plantings. There's a large living room, an ample-size dining room with space for a gaming table, and a brick terrace where a full breakfast is served in good weather. The seven attractive rooms, with a mixture of antiques and reproductions, have private baths, TV, Internet access, and air-conditioning, and some rooms have fireplaces. There's a very large TV in an upstairs sitting room. It's a short walk into town. The B&B is nonsmoking. One-night reservations are accepted.

### Greenwood House
*40 Greenwood Avenue*
*(508) 693–6150, (866) 693–6150*
*www.greenwoodhouse.com*
*Open year-round. Moderate.*

With country-casual furnishings and ample-size rooms, this small inn a few blocks from the town center is a lovely, quiet spot. They provide cable TV, air-conditioning, private baths, telephones, and refrigerators in each room. They also serve a full breakfast. The inn is nonsmoking.

### Causeway Harborview
*124 Skiff Avenue*
*(508) 693–1606*
*Open year-round. Inexpensive.*

Families with children will welcome this sprawling, very plain, informal, motel-type complex, which is on the edge of town, but within walking distance. The apartments and cottages all have fully equipped kitchen units, private baths, and TVs. An ample-size pool overlooks Vineyard Haven Harbor in the distance, and laundry facilities are available on the property.

### Mansion House
*9 Main Street*
*(508) 693–2200, (800) 332–4112*
*www.mvmansionhouse.com*
*Open year-round. Moderate to expensive.*

The successful rebirth of the Mansion House (formerly called the Tisbury Inn before the current owners reclaimed its original name) attests to the fact that this Island landmark has always managed to survive. Dating back to 1794, it was rebuilt after burning to the ground in

1883. The hotel was damaged by another disastrous fire in December 2001, but has since been restored. Visitors are offered state-of-the-art facilities in an atmosphere of Victorian elegance.

Twelve of the thirty-two rooms are suites, many with balconies looking out on Vineyard Haven Harbor. Decorated in cheerful flower prints and peach, green, and other light colors, the rooms have queen- and king-size beds. All of them have air-conditioning, telephones, cable TV, high-speed Internet access, refrigerators, and a coffeemaker. Some have fireplaces and soaking tubs. There is a wheelchair-accessible room on each of the three floors. A state-of-the-art health club has a 75-foot chlorine-free swimming pool. Conference rooms are available for private parties.

A full breakfast is served at their fine restaurant, Zephrus, and lovely shops occupy the ground floor.

### The 1720 House
*152 Main Street*
*(508) 693–6407*
*www.1720house.com*
*Open year-round. Inexpensive.*

This informal farmhouse with low ceilings, a mixture of antique, contemporary, and collectible furnishings, and six small rooms is for the visitor who wants an inexpensive spot close to town with a casual, relaxed ambience. They serve a continental breakfast and afternoon tea. The house also has a small screened porch and terrace.

### Vineyard Harbor Motel
*60 Beach Road (Box 1690)*
*(508) 693–3334, (877) 693–3334*
*Fax (508) 693–0320*
*www.vineyardharbormotel.com*
*Open year-round. Moderate.*

Right on busy Vineyard Haven Harbor but closed off from its commercial neighbors, this motel is quite private. The rooms are nicely decorated with attractive kitchen alcoves or just refrigerators; TVs; and air-conditioning. The little beach is nice for children, and those under six stay free. There is a three-night minimum in season and two nights off-season.

### High Haven House
*85 Summer Street (P.O. Box 289)*
*(508) 693–9204, (800) 232–9204*
*www.highhavenhousemvy.com*
*Open year-round. Expensive*

A ten-minute walk from downtown, but uphill all the way, is this attractive inn with both single rooms and one- or two-bedroom apartments with full kitchens. The main reception room, which looks out on the swimming pool, and the breakfast room are very nicely furnished. There are antiques everywhere, four-poster beds, phones, cable TV, refrigerators, and coffeemakers in all rooms. There's also an aerobic-exercise room for adults. Children are welcome.

# West Tisbury

This farming community, which cuts across the middle of the Island, is about a twenty-minute drive from the Down-Island towns. It has beaches for residents on the north and south shores and is a charming scenic area with several riding stables. It has few places to stay other than private homes. A car is a necessity here. The town is dry, so bring your own alcoholic beverages.

### The Bayberry
*Old Courthouse Road*
*West Tisbury (P.O. Box 546, Vineyard Haven)*
*(508) 693–1984*
*www.mvbayberry.vineyard.net*
*Open year-round. Bed-and-breakfast. Moderate.*

Tucked away in a meadow just off State Road in North Tisbury, the inn is a small, antiques-filled New England bed-and-breakfast spot. The three bedrooms have bright, flowered wallpapers and antique furnishings. The paneled dining room, with its fireplace and nineteenth-century ambience, opens onto a charming terrace where a full complimentary breakfast of blueberry waffles, gingerbread pancakes, or other specialties is served. The owner makes lovely hooked rugs and gives lessons in the winter. Beaches, tennis, and horseback riding are nearby. Bring your own alcoholic beverages. Nonsmoking.

### Lambert's Cove Inn
*Lambert's Cove Road (RR1 422)*
*(508) 693–2298*
*www.lambertscoveinn.com*
*Open year-round. Moderate to expensive.*

This charming inn measures up to one's expectations in every way. The original part of the house was built in 1790 and was greatly enlarged with a barn and carriage house. There are fifteen beautifully decorated rooms with private bathrooms, a large library, and attractive dining rooms. There's a large brick terrace and a gazebo that lend themselves to this ideal setting for weddings. The grounds are lovely and include a tennis court. Full complimentary breakfast is served. Dinner, which is open to the public seasonally by reservation, is also offered. This is a nonsmoking property. Bring your own alcoholic beverages.

# Chilmark

Having your own means of transportation is a must if you stay in Chilmark. Distances are great to the beaches, restaurants, or grocers, and it's a half-hour drive to the Down-Island towns. There are few places to stay other than private homes. The Chilmark Community Center at Beetlebung Corner is the one gathering place. Like West Tisbury, Chilmark is a dry town.

### The Captain R. Flanders House
*North Road*
*(508) 645–3123*
*www.captainflanders.com*
*Seasonal. Inexpensive to moderate.*

Surrounded by rolling fields framed by magnificent stone walls, a windmill, and a pond down in the valley, this eighteenth-century farmhouse built by whaling captain Richard Flanders is a period-piece delight. There are eight rooms, a wonderful eighteenth-century house nearby (available by the week), and two charming little one-bedroom buildings on the property, one with a fireplace. It's a popular spot for weddings, and there's a charming gift shop in the barn that's filled with antiques, china, and glassware. They do not allow weddings in July and August, just spring and fall (May, June, September, and October). A continental breakfast is served on the sunporch, and children older than four are welcome. Nonsmoking inside. Beach passes are provided. Open May to Columbus Day.

### The Inn at Blueberry Hill
*74 North Road*
*(508) 645–3322, (800) 356–3322*
*www.blueberryinn.com*
*Seasonal. Moderate to expensive.*

Attractive simplicity describes this delightful compound surrounded by rolling fields dotted with ancient apple and oak trees, blueberry bushes, and lush gardens framed by stone walls.

There are twenty-five rooms in the main building and three cottages, plus a separate exercise room and a lap pool. Croquet, tennis, and horseshoes are available as well. For those who truly appreciate the quiet joys of country comfort, this inn is delightful. A continental breakfast, box lunch, and dinner (changed daily) are served. Room telephone and TV on request, plus Internet access. Nonsmoking rooms. Bring your own alcoholic beverages. Children twelve and older are welcome. Dinner by reservation to the public. Open May to October.

# Menemsha

### Menemsha Inn and Cottages
*North Road*
*(508) 645–2521*
*www.menemshainn.com*
*Seasonal. Moderate to expensive.*

A dirt road leads off the highway just above Menemsha to this inn, which has a marvelous view of Vineyard Sound and Menemsha. Thirteen efficiency cabins occupy a hillside that stretches down through the meadows and woods to the beach along the north shore. The view of Vineyard Sound from this camplike setting is striking, and the cabins are bright and colorful with fresh paint, crisp curtains, and scatter rugs. They are fully equipped housekeeping units (with the exception of linens). Maid service is provided for those who stay more than a week. Each cabin has its own screened porch, picnic table, outdoor grill, and outdoor shower. Suites and rooms are available in the main building. The inn has twenty-seven rooms in all, its own tennis court, and beach passes are provided. A continental breakfast is served. Nonsmoking. Children welcome. Bring your own alcoholic beverages. Open April to October.

### Beach Plum Inn & Restaurant
*Off North Road*
*(508) 645–9454, (877) 645–7398*
*www.beachpluminn.com*
*Seasonal. Expensive.*

Surrounded by spectacular views of the north shore and Menemsha, this eight-acre compound of cottages and inn is a special spot and one of New England's best.

Most of the ample-size, bright, attractively decorated rooms in the main building have views of the water. The inn has, for years, been a refuge for prominent individuals in government, business, and the arts who want a restful respite. All the rooms have air-conditioning, cable TV, private baths, telephones, and Internet access. The site of many weddings, the entire inn is also available for corporate and university groups.

The amenities are a joy: ocean beaches nearby, a library, fishing boat charters at Menemsha, riding, hiking, tennis, and all the Up-Island country charm at your doorstep. The restaurant is absolutely superb. It serves breakfast to guests and is open to the public for dinner by reservation only. (See Where to Eat chapter.) Children are welcome. Bring your own alcoholic beverages. Open May to December.

# Aquinnah

### Outermost Inn
*Rural Route 1, Box 171*
*Lighthouse Road*
*(508) 645–3511*
*www.outermostinn.com*
*Seasonal. Expensive.*

Located on the high rolling moors on the western tip of the Island, this spectacular site has ocean views in every direction. The seven rooms with private baths have rustic, unpainted furniture in warm wood colors that are most attractive. They serve a full complimentary breakfast, and dinner by reservation is also open to the public. Hugh Taylor, the owner, is a member of the singing Taylor family (James, Kate, and Alex), and guests can sign up for day sails to Cuttyhunk Island on his catamaran. His wife, Jeannie, whose great-great-grandfather was born at the lighthouse, manages this unique hideaway. A car is a necessity except for the short walk to the beautiful ocean beach and the concessions at the cliffs. Bring your own alcoholic beverages.

### Duck Inn
*10 Duck Pond Way, off South Road*
*(508) 645–9018*
*Open year-round. Inexpensive to moderate.*

Rural with breathtaking views overlooking the Atlantic, and extremely casual and cluttered, this small, old seaman's farmhouse is just a step off the main highway going to the cliffs. The bedrooms are small, and the informal living room, dining room, and kitchen are all one large room decorated in Cape Cod, Southwest, Japanese, and Gay Head Duck styles. The inn serves a full breakfast and provides beach lunches, and clambakes can be catered. Duck Inn has a cat and a pig. Children are welcome.

# Campground and Youth Hostel

### Martha's Vineyard Family Campground
*569 Edgartown–Vineyard Haven Road*
*In season (508) 693-3772; off-season (617) 784-3615*
*www.campmv.com*
*Seasonal. Inexpensive.*

This campground, located 1 mile from Vineyard Haven center, is nestled in a grove of oak trees. It accommodates 180 vehicles. The campground allows one motor vehicle, one large tent, or two small tents per site. There's a recreation hall with table tennis, billiards, and other activities; a playground; a ball field; a camp store; bike rentals; and other facilities. No dogs or motorcycles are allowed. Open May to October. Inquire about rates.

### Youth Hostel
*25 West Tisbury Road, West Tisbury*
*(508) 693-2665*
*www.capecodhostels.org*
*Seasonal. Inexpensive.*

Two of West Tisbury's leading citizens, the late Daniel and Lillian Manter, gave this building to the town for a youth hostel. It provides dormitory sleeping, private rooms, and cooking facilities for bicyclists and hikers. The common room is well equipped with books and a fireplace. The hostel is on the Edgartown–Up-Island bike path, 3 miles from the nearest beach. There is a bus stop out front. Nature tours are available. The maximum length of stay is three days in summer and longer in the fall and spring. Space is at a premium, so it is best to make a reservation. Members pay $19 per night per person; nonmembers pay $32 per night per person. Open April to October.

# 7

# WHERE TO EAT

There is a wide variety of places to eat on the Vineyard to suit all tastes and preferences. You'll find elegant and expensive restaurants as well as simple family restaurants, plus many places to get a take-out snack or lunch for a day on the beach or bicycling around the Island. Many places are open spring through fall; almost all Up-Island places are closed in winter.

You may find the less expensive places quite crowded during the busiest time of midsummer, so it's advisable to plan ahead if possible. Some of the more expensive places prefer that you make reservations, and proprietors prefer to have their guests appropriately dressed, with the men in jackets and the women in dressy slacks or dresses; this is particularly true in Edgartown, which is more formal than the other towns. Be sure to inquire about payment when making a reservation; some restaurants take only certain credit cards, and others won't accept personal checks.

The general price categories for restaurants listed in this chapter are as follows: expensive, $35 or more per entree, depending on what is included; moderate, $20 to $34; and inexpensive, $10 to $19. A moderate-to-expensive range usually means that the lunch is moderate in cost while the dinner might be $25 or more; inexpensive-to-moderate implies the same kind of price variation. These prices will vary a bit, depending on the extras one might order, and all are subject to fluctuations in the market prices for lobster and swordfish. Those places suitable for children are noted. Others are listed under "Family Restaurants and Takeout."

# Edgartown

### *The Terrace*
*The Charlotte Inn*
*27 South Summer Street*
*(508) 627–4751*
*Seasonal. Expensive.*

The Terrace, a new restaurant in a familiar location at the Charlotte Inn, is one of the Island's best. The pleasant art gallery setting is surrounded by lush, cool gardens and a fountain. It is a charming backdrop for the excellent fish cuisine touched with an Italian flair, the lamb, grilled beef, and other original entrees. The wines are superb, and everything is beautifully served.

The restaurant serves lunch and dinner daily in season and on limited nights off-season. Reservations are necessary.

### *The Grill on Main*
*227 Upper Main Street*
*(508) 627–8344*
*www.thegrillonmain.com*
*Open year-round. Expensive.*

There is a subtle charm to this dining spot with its casual, upscale ambience. There's an attractive alcove bar, the tables are appropriately spaced for comfort, and the decorative paintings are charming. It is one of the Island's best restaurants. The fish, poultry, and beef entrees are innovative and delicious. Located next to the Stop & Shop grocer, there is ample parking in the rear.

### L'Etoile

*22 North Water Street*
*(508) 627–5187*
*www.letoile.net*
*Seasonal. Expensive*

Formerly in the Charlotte Inn, this superb restaurant is in a new location across from Mudge's Candy Store. The delicious tasting menu choices include fish, lamb, and beef entrees. It is one of the Island's best dining options. It seats fifty comfortably, and there's a bar in the back.

### Detente

*3 Nevin Square*
*Winter Street*
*(508) 627–8810*
*FAX (508) 627–4977*
*www.detentewinebar.com*
*Seasonal. Expensive.*

This delightfully quiet, hidden spot is very simply decorated and has seating for fifty-five. Their simplicity belies the superb menu, which is a fusion of French and Italian themes and ingredients. The owners have experience working at several fine Island restaurants and have struck out on their own with this one. It's a winner, and the wines are very special.

### The Coach House

*The Harborview Hotel*
*131 North Water Street*
*(508) 627–3761*
*www.harbor-view.com/coach_house*
*Open year-round. Moderate to expensive.*

The turn-of-the-twentieth-century Harborview Hotel is a treasure. Its dining room has a sweeping view of Edgartown's outer harbor and lighthouse. Open for breakfast, lunch, and dinner, the restaurant serves delicious, savory selections of fine native seafood—swordfish, lobster, sole, and quahog chowder—as well as lamb, duckling, and beef.

The bar in the dining room opens at 11:00 A.M. Their cafe, the Breezes, also open year-round, is attractive, and guests can take their appetizers, salads, and sandwiches, as well as drinks, out to the porch to enjoy the colorful boating activity in the harbor. Wheelchair accessible. Ample parking. Suitable for older children.

### The Square Rigger
*235 State Road*
*(508) 627-9968*
*www.members.tripod.com/squarerigger*
*Open year-round. Expensive to very expensive.*

This old house at the fork in the road on State Road has been a restaurant for years. An Island favorite, it has a tavern ambience with its plain wood tables, captain's chairs, old beams, and a long bar.

Year after year it is known for delicious steak and seafood specialties that are charbroiled on an open hearth; the lobster choices are exceptional. It is arguably the best seafood restaurant on the Island. Dinner nightly from 6:00 P.M. Wheelchair accessible. Takeout also available.

### The Wharf
*Lower Main Street*
*(508) 627-9966*
*Open year-round. Moderate.*

This pub and restaurant, located near the waterfront, is a favorite with the Island's year-round residents. There's a sports bar adjacent to the dining area and live entertainment. They specialize in fish entrees that are tasty and nicely served. Open for lunch and dinner.

### Atria

*137 Main Street*
*(508) 627–5850*
*www.atriamv.com*
*Seasonal. Expensive.*

This is one of the Island's best restaurants, and the dining room, which seats one hundred, is bright and cheerful. The downstairs lounge, with its brick walls and old wooden beams, is the perfect setting for soft, sophisticated jazz, and they serve light fare. There is a bar out in the garden on summer evenings.

The food is superb and the chef often adds an Asian touch to traditional New England fish and local organic vegetables. Reservations preferred. Atria is a gourmet delight. Dinners only and weekend brunches. Wheelchair accessible. Open May to January.

### Espresso Love

*2 South Water Street*
*Post Office Square*
*(508) 627–9211*
*Seasonal. Moderate.*

This bright little spot, with its metal umbrella tables in a garden setting, gives no clue to the fact that it is also a superb caterer and one of the Island's top restaurants.

They serve delicious breakfasts, lunches, and dinners both indoors and on the terrace. Suitable for children on the terrace. Wheelchair accessible.

### The English Butler Tea Room

*22 Winter Street*
*(508) 627–1013*
*www.unitedkingdomtea.com*
*Seasonal. Moderate.*

A century ago tearooms were very popular in Edgartown. Thanks to the charming English couple that owns this place, there is now a wonderful one here once more, serving many, many varieties of tea, scones, real clotted cream, and delightful pastries. It's very British and a very sophisticated addition to Edgartown's gourmet scene. Closed midwinter.

### Seafood Shanty

*31 Dock Street*
*(508) 627–8622*
*www.theseafoodshanty.com*
*Seasonal. Moderate.*

Overlooking the harbor with sensational views of the waterfront, this is an old favorite for many. The savory seafood specialties at this restaurant are very popular. An Island landmark for years, it's open for lunch and dinner during the season. The restaurant also has entertainment and serves light fare in the pub upstairs, which is open from 3:00 to 10:00 P.M. Wheelchair accessible. Children's menu.

### Lattanzi's

*Old Post Office Square*
*(508) 627–8854*
*Fax (508) 627–9085*
*www.lattanzis.com*
*Open year-round. Inexpensive to expensive.*

Lattanzi's comes in three parts: the handsomely furnished, more formal, expensive restaurant with antique reproduction furniture, brass fixtures, a fireplace, and fresh flowers; the adjacent Lattanzi's Pizzeria, which is less formal than the restaurant; and a seasonal take-out spot with

Good Day to you!
My name is Dobson: R___ ___t (Retired).
Do stop for a chat and ___ picture...
Then drop a quarter ___ pitcher.
(They work me like ___ dog, you know.)
Thank you!

*The butler's greeting at the door of the*
*English Butler Tea Room.*

sandwiches in the back, facing Church Street. The pizzeria has a fireplace and a large brick oven where the savory pizzas are cooked. The pizzas can be eaten inside or out on the porch tables. Reservations are not necessary.

In the formal dining room, which is charming, they serve familiar pork, lamb, fish, and beef selections, which have all been prepared in the chef's original, creative manner and are a gourmet's delight. Open for dinner year-round. Reservations preferred. Wheelchair accessible.

### Alchemy
*71 Main Street*
*(508) 627–9999*
*Fax (508) 627–7503*
*Open year-round. Moderate to expensive.*

Alchemy has had a reputation for fine food for years and is owned by the same people who own Espresso Love, which is just around the corner. The first floor is attractively decorated, and there are a few tables outside. The small balcony upstairs overlooks Main Street.

### The Newes from America
*Kelley House*
*23 Kelley Street*
*(508) 627–4397*
*www.kelley-house.com/dining.shtml*
*Open year-round. Inexpensive to moderate.*

The eighteenth-century, tavernlike character of this Kelley House hotel pub, with its exposed original beams and brick walls, makes it a delightful spot for a light lunch or dinner. Located in the center of town, it's adjacent to, but not on, the harbor. The clam chowder, salads, lobster rolls, and other familiar choices are quite tasty. Open year-round for lunch and dinner daily. Wheelchair accessible. Reservations not required.

# Oak Bluffs

### Lola's Southern Seafood
*Beach Road*
*(508) 693–5007*
*www.lolassouthernseafood.com*
*Open year-round. Inexpensive to moderate.*

Adjacent to the Island Inn, Lola's has a large dining area and a pub that serves light fare along with lively, rambunctious entertainment. It is a popular nightspot. The specialty here, char-grilled Southern seafood, is a favorite of patrons, as are the other New Orleans–style dinners. Lola's also serves a breakfast buffet seasonally and has a fine children's menu. Full bar, ample parking, and wheelchair accessible.

### Offshore Ale Co.
*35 Kennebec Avenue*
*(508) 693–2626*
*www.offshoreale.com*
*Open year-round. Inexpensive.*

This restaurant a step away from Circuit Avenue makes its own distinctive beer right on the premises, the vats visible on the balcony. The tavernlike dark wall paneling, booths, and tables are the ideal background for the moderately priced, fine food and the various home brews. It's a lively spot with music most nights. Open 5:00 P.M. to midnight daily. Wheelchair accessible.

### Pomodoro
*53 Circuit Avenue*
*(508) 696–3002*
*Open year-round. Moderate.*

This is a very handsome building with carefully spaced tables and rich, period-piece wooden booths. It makes an attractive, relaxing backdrop for the many Italian entrees as well as the large selection of pizzas. Lunch and dinner are served.

### Nancy's
*29 Lake Avenue*
*Oak Bluffs Harbor*
*(508) 693–0006*
*Fax (508) 693–5858*
*www.nancysrestaurant.com*
*Open May to mid-September. Inexpensive to expensive.*

Nancy's has been on the harbor for over forty years, and it's huge. There's a snack bar on the dock, and upstairs there's a large dining room looking out on the harbor and an open deck. There is a large menu to suit all: It varies from fried seafood, sandwiches, salads, and Middle Eastern specialties to traditional beef and fish entrees.

### Bangkok Cuisine
*67 Circuit Avenue*
*(508) 696–6322*
*Open year-round. Moderate.*

This delightful new restaurant is a fine addition to the Oak Bluffs culinary scene. Located in an old Victorian house, it seats about fifty. The various Thai choices are unusual and very different from most Island restaurants. Rice is a staple, with curry and other sauces, Thai spices, plus many original sauces for the chicken, fish, or pork entrees.

### Lookout Tavern
*8 Seaview Avenue Extension*
*(508) 696–9844*
*Seasonal. Inexpensive to moderate.*

This extremely popular tavern is right across the street from the beach and the Steamship Authority pier. Oblong tables accommodate as many as possible, plus there are tables on the porch and a bar. They offer a huge sushi menu, a raw bar, wraps, sandwiches, and salads, which are quite good. Open daily 11:00 A.M. to 11:00 P.M.

### The Captain's Table
*5 Oak Bluffs Avenue*
*(508) 696–0220*
*Open year-round. Inexpensive to moderate.*

A stone's throw from the Woods Hole Ferry, this diner is a favorite spot for Island residents and visitors alike. There's a traditional counter and a few tables. The fish and beef dinners are under $30 and are very tasty. It is open daily in season for breakfast, lunch, and dinner. In the off-season, it is only open on weekends for dinner.

## Along the Boardwalk

On the dock at Oak Bluffs harbor, there are five restaurants with a wide variety of culinary selections, a couple of gift shops, and the site of the Monster Shark Tournament and Seafood Festival.

### Farm Neck Golf Club Cafe
*County Road*
*(508) 693–3560*
*Seasonal. Moderate.*

There are three sunporch dining rooms in this attractive setting overlooking the Farm Neck Golf Course. The moderately priced food is very good, and the lunch menu is quite large. Beer and wine are available. They serve breakfast and lunch from April to November, and dinner from June through September. Closed Mondays.

### Season's Eatery and Pub

*19 Circuit Avenue*
*(508) 693–7129*
*www.seasonseatery.com*
*Open year-round. Inexpensive.*

Season's swings with its live entertainment, sixteen TV screens, cocktail lounge, and inexpensive food. Wheelchair accessible.

# Vineyard Haven

There are many small indoor and outdoor cafes along Vineyard Haven's Main Street that all have takeout. They vary in their selections of pizzas, sandwiches, subs, and pastries. There is usually a small courtyard of outdoor tables for those places that are takeout-only.

### The Black Dog Tavern

*Beach Street Extension*
*(508) 693–9223*
*www.theblackdog.com/tavern.aspx*
*Open year-round. Moderate to expensive.*

Restless children can play on the beach while waiting for meals to be served in this well-known eatery on Vineyard Haven Harbor, with its waterfront-tavern ambience. The dinners they serve put particular emphasis on local fish, and there's a nice array of simple selections for children. Open for breakfast, lunch, and dinner, with dinner served from 5:00 to 10:00 P.M. Bring your own alcoholic beverages. No reservations.

### Mediterranean Restaurant

*52 Beach Road*
*(508) 693–1617, (888) 693–1617*
*Fax (508) 693–7877*
*Seasonal. Moderate to expensive.*

Tucked between two commercial buildings is this quiet little spot on the harbor. The chef was formerly with the Black Dog, and most of the recipes are based on rustic peasant dishes from the western Mediterranean: Spanish, Greek, North African, and Provençal. The selections are delicious and attract a loyal following.

The restaurant is two stories high with an open porch on the second floor affording a delightful view of the harbor. BYOB.

### Le Grenier French Restaurant
*Main Street*
*(508) 693–4906*
*www.legrenierrestaurant.com*
*Open year-round. Expensive.*

This is Vineyard Haven's premier restaurant and one of the Island's best. The chef and owner, from Lyon, France, is imaginative and creates both delicate and delicious French food. Some of the unusual selections are not found in any other Island restaurants. The room seats ninety, and the pastel linens, candlelit tables, and skylights provide an attractive atmosphere. Dinner and Sunday brunch are the only meals served here. Located upstairs and open year-round except for a short period during midwinter. Reservations are required. You may bring your own alcoholic beverages.

### Zephrus
*Main Street*
*(508) 693–3416*
*www.mvmansionhouse.com/zephrus.html*
*Open year-round. Inexpensive to expensive.*

The Mansion House's popular restaurant is attractively designed with indoor and outdoor seating. Seafood specialties are featured, and their pastries with afternoon tea are delicious. Sandwiches are $10 or less. They serve breakfast, lunch, and dinner, and it's all very good. BYOB.

# West Tisbury

### *Lambert's Cove Inn*

*Lambert's Cove Road*

*(508) 693–2298*

*www.lambertscoveinn.com/restaurant.html*

*Open year-round. Moderate to expensive.*

This charming country inn, with an attractive porch looking out on an old apple orchard, has been featured in *Gourmet* magazine. The fine dinner selections include lamb, beef, veal, and fish. Both the porch and the large sitting room with fireplace are relaxed and comfortable places to gather before going in to dinner. Dinner is served daily in the summer and on weekends during the rest of the year. Reservations are requested. Bring your own alcoholic beverages.

# Chilmark

### *At the Cornerway Restaurant*

*13 State Road*

*(508) 645–9300*

*www.atthecornerway.com*

*Seasonal. Expensive.*

Located in the center of Chilmark, this is a favorite dinner spot for Up-Island vacationers. It has a relaxed atmosphere, with spacious seating, contemporary furniture, and art-decorated walls.

Although it is not open for lunch, the restaurant is available for private parties anytime. Open May to October. Reservations suggested. Bring your own alcoholic beverages. Wheelchair accessible.

### Theo's

*The Inn at Blueberry Hill*
*North Road*
*(508) 645-3322*
*www.blueberryinn.com/theos.htm*
*Seasonal. Expensive.*

Charming simplicity with a blue-and-yellow motif, Hitchcock chairs, and a windowed veranda looking out on a pastoral setting defines the dining room in this country inn, which seats fifty. The delightful gourmet dinners are changed nightly. Open nightly to the public from 7:00 to 9:30 P.M., May to November, by reservation. Bring your own liquor.

# Menemsha

### Homeport

*512 North Road*
*(508) 645-2679*
*Seasonal. Moderate to expensive.*

Overlooking Menemsha Creek, which runs from the harbor into Menemsha Pond, this casual eating place has long been known for its excellent fresh seafood. It's an Island institution, and for years people from the Down-Island towns have brought their cocktails to drink out on the stone jetty or Menemsha Beach and then enjoyed a seafood dinner at Homeport. Open on a seasonal basis for dinner only; reservations necessary. Wheelchair accessible. Suitable for children. Bring your own liquor.

### Beach Plum Inn Restaurant

*Off North Road*
*(508) 645–9454*
*www.beachpluminn.com/restaurant.htm*
*Seasonal. Expensive.*

This is a very special spot and an extraordinary gourmet delight. The dining room looks out on Menemsha Harbor and the north shore and is surrounded by a lovely brick terrace, flowers, porches, and lawns, with rolling fields reaching down toward the sea.

The entrees are unusual; the fish selections are innovative and sophisticated (try lobster with caviar). The menu is changed constantly, and the restaurant is open for dinner seven nights a week (after October 1, five nights) and seats eighty-five. Open to the public; reservations required. Bring your own alcoholic beverages. Open May to December.

# Aquinnah

### The Aquinnah Shop

*27 Aquinnah Circle*
*Gay Head Cliffs*
*(508) 645–3867*
*Seasonal. Inexpensive to moderate.*

This Island institution is an old favorite, and the tradition of good, inexpensive food for lunch and dinner goes on. They emphasize American cuisine, and the lobster is exceptional. The establishment was originally founded at the beginning of World War II by Napoleon Bonaparte Madison, the Wampanoag tribal medicine man and whaler. It is now run by Ann Vanderhoop, Napoleon's daughter-in-law, and her husband, Luther, who is the current medicine man. It has both takeout and tables inside and out on the deck, which hangs over the sea. It's crowded at noon, when most tour buses stop in the area. Open mid-April to mid-October. Breakfast and lunch menus are original and delicious, and the pies are famous. Wheelchair accessible. BYOB

# Family Restaurants and Takeout

## Edgartown

### Main Street Diner
*Old Post Office Square*
*(508) 627–9337*
*Seasonal. Inexpensive.*

The checkerboard floor and walls decorated with old 1920s beer, Pepsi, Coca-Cola, and cigarette ads set the tone for this perky, reasonably priced eatery. Open daily 7:00 A.M. to 10:00 P.M.; closed mid-January to mid-March. The sandwiches, salads, homemade muffins, bountiful breakfasts, and some special dinners are very tasty. Takeout is also available. Wheelchair accessible.

### Morning Glory Farm
*West Tisbury Road*
*(508) 627–9003*
*Seasonal. Inexpensive.*

About a half mile from the center of Edgartown is another of those wonderful Island institutions. Originally, the owners of the farm, the Athearns, sold just plants, fruits, and vegetables at their little barn. But they have since expanded a great deal, to everyone's delight. They now sell delicious home-baked pastries and pies, cheese, milk, eggs, their own beef and pork, and organic fruits and vegetables. The nice shady lawn is particularly inviting to tired bicyclists to rest and enjoy their food and cold drinks. Open Memorial Day to Christmas.

### Edgartown Pizza

*224 Edgartown Road, at the Triangle*
*(508) 627-7770*
*Open year-round. Inexpensive.*

On Upper Main Street opposite the Square Rigger Restaurant, this inexpensive pizza spot has accessible parking and tables indoors and out on the deck away from the midtown crowds. The pizzas are tasty, as are the sandwiches; they also serve beer, wine, and cordials. It's a great spot for children. Open for lunch and dinner. Wheelchair accessible.

### Fresh Pasta Shoppe

*206 Upper Main Street*
*(508) 627-5582*
*Open year-round. Inexpensive.*

This little spot, across from the Texaco gas station, has what many consider the best pizzas on the Island. Easy parking. Takeout only.

### Pizzeria

*At Lattanzi's*
*Old Post Office Square*
*(508) 627-9084*
*www.lattanzis.com*
*Open year-round. Inexpensive.*

With tables inside and out on the deck, pizzas cooked in brick ovens, and a bright and cheerful decor, this is a great family spot. The pizzas range from those with baby clams, spinach, and other ingredients to the four European cheeses with tomatoes, and they're very tasty. Open Tuesday through Sunday from 5:30 to 11:00 P.M. Wheelchair accessible.

### Dairy Queen

*242 Main Street (opposite Stop & Shop)*
*(508) 627–5001*
*Seasonal. Inexpensive.*

After the usual quiet winter in Edgartown, the store's April opening is a great treat for children. They have all the ice-cream favorites, hot dogs, and birthday cakes.

### Humphrey's of Edgartown

*32 Winter Street*
*(508) 627–7029*
*Seasonal. Inexpensive.*

Humphrey's in West Tisbury was an Island institution for many, many years, and people still talk about Archie, the owner of the original establishment. A new generation now runs an inspired store in Edgartown, which is well known for its pastries and large sandwiches.

# Oak Bluffs

### Ocean View Restaurant and Cocktail Lounge

*16 Chapman Avenue*
*(508) 693–2207*
*Open year-round. Inexpensive to moderate.*

This popular family restaurant is located near the harbor. It is paneled and has amply spaced square wooden tables and a nice tavern room. The food is good, with many Island fish selections. Lunch and dinner are served daily, and reservations are required for six or more guests. There are plenty of parking spaces. Children are welcome. Wheelchair accessible.

### Linda Jean's Restaurant

*25 Circuit Avenue*

*(508) 693–4093*

*Open year-round. Inexpensive.*

The homemade food at Linda Jean's, a favorite breakfast spot of Island residents, is very good, as are the hamburgers, sandwiches, and desserts served at lunchtime. This restaurant is extremely popular. Open from 6:00 A.M. to 8:00 P.M. daily. Bring your own alcoholic beverages.

### Slice of Life

*50 Circuit Avenue*

*(508) 693–3838*

*Open year-round. Moderate.*

A few steps across the street from Sun Porch Book Store is the popular Slice of Life. Their bakery-deli selections are excellent. Takeout is offered and there are a few tables for dining on the premises.

# Vineyard Haven

### M. V. Bagel Authority

*96 Main Street*

*(508) 693–4152*

*Open year-round. Inexpensive.*

Bagels have finally come to the Island in full force, and this attractive indoor-outdoor cafe is located just across from the stone bank on Upper Main Street. The bagels are fine, and the place has become popular for breakfast and lunch, which includes sandwiches and salads. The street-side porch is very popular in summer. Wheelchair accessible.

### Art Cliff Diner
*39 Beach Road*
*(508) 693-1224*
*Open year-round. Inexpensive.*

This very popular neighborhood diner is a favorite with local residents, some of whom gather each morning to gossip and discuss town affairs. It seats forty and has a very large and varied breakfast menu, and the tasty lunch menu has a nice selection of crepes, salads, and sandwiches, all for under $15.

### Louis' Tisbury Eatery
*350 State Road*
*(508) 693-3255*
*Open year-round. Inexpensive.*

For over twenty years Louis' has been a favorite delicatessen for Islanders. The plain brown shingled building across from Cronig's Market gives no clue to the salads, cold meats, sandwiches, and other take-out foods, including soups and pastries, available within. There is a large selection, which can be eaten inside or outside at the picnic tables.

### The Black Dog Bakery Cafe
*157 State Road*
*(508) 696-8190*
*www.theblackdog.com*
*Seasonal. Moderate.*

On the outskirts of town and with convenient parking, this bakery is an offshoot of the original Black Dog Cafe. Opening at 6:30 A.M., they serve a fine breakfast and lunch Monday through Saturday. Dinner is served Wednesday through Saturday until 9:00 P.M. Bring your own alcoholic beverages.

# West Tisbury

### Garcia's Bakery and Deli
*West Tisbury Center*
*(508) 693–4095*
*Open year-round. Inexpensive.*
Behind the famous Alley's Store, which sells everything from pots to pickles, is a nice spot to pick up some delicious sandwiches and pastries. They have a couple of picnic tables, and the adjacent parking lot is most convenient.

# Chilmark

### Chilmark Store
*7 State Road*
*Beetlebung Corner*
*(508) 645–3739*
*Seasonal. Inexpensive.*

Located in the center of Chilmark, this country store has a take-out section that offers twenty-five kinds of delicious pizzas and sandwiches. They will take orders for those who want to pick up their food on their way to or from the beach. This is a rare find at the western end of the Island, where there are few places to eat, and it is very popular.

# Menemsha

### *The Menemsha Deli*
*24 Basin Road*
*(508) 645–9902*
*Seasonal. Inexpensive.*

Menemsha is Chilmark's port, and there are a couple of places to eat here. This deli offers tasty soups, salads, sandwiches, and desserts that can be eaten at picnic tables or taken to the town beach nearby. Bring your own alcoholic beverages.

### *Menemsha Galley*
*515 North Road, Menemsha Harbor*
*(508) 645–9819*
*Seasonal. Inexpensive.*

For over fifty years the famous and the average citizen alike have stopped by this little food stand at the base of the harbor. They serve hamburgers, hot dogs, lobster sandwiches, clam chowder, and other summertime fare. In the back there's a little porch facing the harbor. It was a favorite spot for the late *Life* magazine photographer Alfred Eisenstaedt.

# 8

# TELEPHONE NUMBERS AND ADDRESSES

Here are some important telephone numbers and addresses for your basic needs during your Island vacation or to answer your questions before you visit the Island.

## General

For *emergency* only—fire, police, or ambulance, dial 911

**Martha's Vineyard Hospital,** Hospital Road, Oak Bluffs, (508) 693-0410

**Massachusetts State Police,** Temihigan Avenue, Oak Bluffs, (508) 693-0545

**Aquinnah Police Headquarters,** State Road, Chilmark, (508) 645-2313

**Chilmark Police Headquarters,** Beetlebung Corner, (508) 645-3310

**Edgartown Police Headquarters,** Church Street, (508) 627-4343

**Oak Bluffs Police Headquarters,** Oak Bluffs Avenue (ferry wharf), (508) 693-0750

**Vineyard Haven (Tisbury) Police Headquarters,** town parking lot, (508) 696-4240

**West Tisbury Police Headquarters,** State Road, (508) 693-0020

**U.S. Coast Guard,** Menemsha Station, (508) 645-2611

**Animal Health Care,** Martha's Vineyard Airport, (508) 693-6515

**Massachusetts SPCA,** Vineyard Haven Road, Edgartown, (508) 627-8662

**Dukes County Courthouse,** Edgartown, (508) 627-3751

# Churches

### Edgartown

**Assembly of God,** 258 Edgartown–Vineyard Haven Road, (508) 627–7926

**Edgartown United Methodist Church** (Old Whaling Church), 89 Main Street, (508) 627–4442

**Faith Community Church,** 231 Meeting House Way, (508) 627–8918

**First Federated Church,** South Summer Street, (508) 627–4421

**St. Andrew's Episcopal Church,** North Summer Street, (508) 627–5330

**St. Elizabeth's Roman Catholic Church,** 86 Main Street, (508) 627–5017

### Oak Bluffs

**Apostolic House of Prayer,** Pequot Avenue, (508) 696–9916

**Christ United Methodist Church,** 64 Washington Avenue, (508) 693–0576

**Christian Science Society,** 123 New York Avenue, (508) 696–7369

**St. Augustine's Church,** 55 School Street, (508) 693–0342

**The Tabernacle** (interdenominational), Campground, (508) 693–0525

**Trinity Episcopal Church,** East Chop Drive, (508) 693–3780

**Trinity Methodist Church,** Campground, (508) 693–0589

**Union Chapel** (interdenominational), Kennebec and Circuit Avenue, (508) 693–5350

### Vineyard Haven

**Assembly of God,** 1048 State Road, (508) 696–7576

**Christ United Methodist Church,** Church Street, (508) 693–0476

First Baptist Church, 43 Spring Street, (508) 693–1539

Grace Episcopal Church, Woodlawn Avenue, (508) 693–0332

Martha's Vineyard Hebrew Center, Center Street, (508) 693–0745

St. Augustine's Roman Catholic Church, Franklin Street, (508) 693–0103

The Unitarian Universalist Society of Martha's Vineyard, Main Street, (508) 693–8982

### West Tisbury

First Congregational Church, West Tisbury Center, (508) 693–2842

Jehovah's Witnesses, 48 State Road, (508) 693–6356

### Chilmark

Chilmark United Methodist Church, Menemsha Crossroads, (508) 645–3100

### Aquinnah

Community Baptist Church, Aquinnah Center, (508) 693–1539

# Conservation Organizations

There are nine conservation organizations on the Island, and all are working feverishly to acquire and protect the remaining open land. Thirty percent of the Island landmass is now under conservation restrictions, and each year conservation groups seem to acquire a bit more land. The rules and regulations for protected land vary; some permit swimming, fishing, and/or boating; all permit nature walks. There are walking trails in all six towns.

Six conservation organizations are located at the Wakeman Conservation Center on Lambert's Cove Road (Vineyard Haven; 508–693–7233). There you can get detailed information on conservation lands open to the public and on the following organizations: Martha's Vineyard Garden Club, Sheriff's Meadow Foundation, Trustees of Reservations, Vineyard Conservation Society, Nature Conservancy, Vineyard Open Land Foundation, and Marsh Hawk Land Trust, Inc.

# Visitor Information

The Martha's Vineyard Chamber of Commerce is helpful in answering general questions about the Island. It is located on Beach Road in Vineyard Haven, around the corner from the ferry wharf. The telephone number is (508) 693–0085 and the Web address is www.mvy.com. You may write to them at P.O. Box 1698, Vineyard Haven, MA 02568.

All three Down-Island towns have visitor information centers: in Edgartown on Church Street behind the Whaling Church, in Oak Bluffs by the merry-go-round, and in Vineyard Haven at the ferry parking lot.

# Historical Information

The Martha's Vineyard Museum, on School Street in Edgartown, is the Island's main museum. The exhibits are fascinating and change from time to time. The staff there are helpful in answering questions about the Vineyard's history, as well as genealogical queries. The museum publishes an excellent historical quarterly, the *Dukes County Intelligencer,* which is on sale at their offices along with other publications on the history of the Vineyard. Financial contributions are always welcome should any visitor care to subscribe to the quarterly or give directly to the museum. The telephone number is (508) 627–4441.

# Libraries

Aquinnah Public Library, Aquinnah Center, (508) 645–2314

Chilmark Public Library, Chilmark Center, (508) 645–3360

Edgartown Public Library, North Water Street, (508) 627–4221

Gale Huntington Library, Martha's Vineyard Historical Society, School Street, Edgartown, (508) 627–4441

Oak Bluffs Public Library, 56R School Street, (508) 693–9433

Vineyard Haven Public Library, Main Street, (508) 696–4210

West Tisbury Public Library, South Road, (508) 693–3366

# Museums

Aquinnah Cultural Center (Wampanoag Museum), 35 Aquinnah Circle, Aquinnah, (508) 645–7900

Cottage Museum, Campground, Oak Bluffs (contact the Martha's Vineyard Campmeeting Association at 508–693–0525)

The Firehouse Museum, Edgartown, (no phone)

The Martha's Vineyard Museum, School Street, Edgartown, (508) 627–4441

# Post Offices and Zip Codes

**Aquinnah** (Chilmark post office and code)

**Chilmark,** Beetlebung Corner, (508) 645–2535; 02535

**Edgartown,** Upper Main Street, (508) 627–7318; 02539

**Menemsha,** Menemsha Market Substation, (508) 645–3501; 02552
(open May 15 to September 15)

**Oak Bluffs,** Park Avenue, (508) 693–1049; 02557

**Vineyard Haven,** Lagoon Pond Road, (508) 693–2818; 02568

**West Tisbury,** State Road, (508) 693–7899; 02575

## The Mailroom

Whether you're mailing something as large as a bicycle or as small as a jar of jelly, the Mailroom will take care of it for you. They will ship anything via UPS or FedEx. They also offer business services such as photocopying and sending and receiving faxes, and you can log on to the Internet and read your e-mail. It is a great convenience for those on vacation as well as Island residents. The Mailroom is located in the Triangle Plaza at 243 Edgartown Road in Edgartown (508-627-7704; www.mailroom.vineyard.net).

# Translation Services

If you are a foreigner and need help with your English, contact or visit the chamber of commerce on Beach Street in Vineyard Haven, (508) 693–0085.

# Public Restrooms

Public restrooms are located in the following places:

**Aquinnah,** near the parking lot at the cliffs

**Edgartown,** at the visitor center on Church Street, the town hall, and the changing rooms at South Beach

**Menemsha,** across from the fish market

**Oak Bluffs,** next to the Steamship Authority terminal, near the post office, and at the harbor next to Our Market

**Vineyard Haven,** at the Steamship Authority, in the Stop & Shop parking lot, and behind the fire station on Beach Road

**West Tisbury,** at the Grange Hall building next to the town hall

# 9

# LEISURE ACTIVITIES

It is difficult to imagine any leisure activities that are *not* available to Island visitors. Enjoy the outdoors while hiking, biking, bird-watching, kayaking, sailing, or fly fishing. Play croquet on a professional croquet lawn (next to the Edgartown School or at a tournament on a private court), try your hand at tennis, or play a round of golf. Water-sports enthusiasts will discover opportunities for windsurfing, parasailing, tube riding, and wake-boarding. Explore your artistic side by taking lessons in dance, music, theater, photography, painting, quilting, or jewelry making. Take a walking tour of historical or wildlife sites or visit galleries and museums. Enjoy the many plays, concerts, films, and lectures scheduled throughout the summer. Watch or participate in a variety of road races and regattas. Charter a boat for a daylong fishing excursion or a sunset cruise. Read on for more details about the many activities available to you on Martha's Vineyard.

## Antiques Shops

Browsing in antiques shops is a favorite pastime for many Island visitors. You will find antiques and collectibles for sale in all the towns except Aquinnah. The prices and quality vary a great deal, from simple collectibles to country pine furniture, china, early American brasses, turn-of-the-twentieth-century wicker, and nineteenth-century furniture and reproductions.

# Art Galleries

Many art galleries in the Island towns feature photographs and paintings. Island scenes in watercolors and prints predominate, but the variety is enormous, from the least expensive lighthouse print to works by well-known artists whose work has been featured in art galleries in New York, Boston, and other urban art centers.

# Art Instruction

Many art galleries provide instruction for both children and adults. There are also many individuals and groups that offer instruction in handcrafts, photography, and papermaking. It is best to check with the chamber of commerce or the individual galleries.

### Featherstone Center for the Arts
*30 Featherstone Lane, Oak Bluffs*
*(508) 693–1850*
*www.featherstonearts.org*

This organization offers many disciplines in the arts and is open year-round. They provide instruction in poetry writing, art, jewelry making, photography, music, tapestry, pottery making, and many other classes for children and adults. It was founded a little over ten years ago and has become a very successful nonprofit organization with gallery shows and concerts.

# Beaches

The Island beaches are very popular with summer and fall visitors. The gently lapping waves all along the north and northeast sound side of the Island are ideal for swimming or launching a sailboard. Some of these beaches are pebbly, while others are wide and sandy. The Atlantic Ocean beaches have fine sand in most places and coarse sand in a few others. The size of the surf depends on the weather conditions. Many beaches are open to the general public, but a number of town beaches are open to residents and guests only.

At times the ocean surf along the south shore from Chappaquiddick to Aquinnah can be rough, with a strong undertow that's dangerous. Vacationers are advised to be cautious and talk with the lifeguards if necessary. Deer ticks, which can cause Lyme disease, are found in the beach grasses, so it's best to stay away from them.

## Chappaquiddick

Cape Pogue Wildlife Refuge and Wasque Reservation, two adjoining beaches on Chappaquiddick Island, run along the east side of the Island. They are managed by the Trustees of Reservations and are subject to their regulations. To reach the beach, take the Chappy ferry and go directly across the Island on the only paved road. Then take the Dyke Bridge dirt road at the intersection to Cape Pogue's East Beach or stay on the paved road, which later becomes a dirt road and leads to the Wasque parking lot. The beach is open to all.

## Edgartown

The Lighthouse Beach is at the entrance to Edgartown Harbor, by the lighthouse, and is open to all.

Katama Beach, the public beach at South Beach, is on the south side of Edgartown. There is a shuttle bus to the beach from the center of town. If you drive here, follow Pease Point Way to the beach, which is 3 miles from town. About 5 blocks from Edgartown's center, there's a fork in the road, and both roads lead to the beach. This ocean beach is extremely popular and has bathhouses for changing, restrooms, and lifeguards. Visitors are constantly asked to pick up their own trash and not to trample or drive on the dunes. Katama, in Indian dialect, means "crab-fishing place."

The Edgartown–Oak Bluffs State Beach (called Joseph A. Sylvia Beach) is a 2-mile stretch of open beach along State Road that runs between Oak Bluffs and Edgartown. It is a fine swimming beach, with some areas more pebbly than others, and it is very popular in midsummer. There are lifeguards at the Edgartown end of the beach, but as on many Island beaches, there are no food stands other than an ice-cream truck at the Oak Bluffs end and no toilet facilities. The beach is open to all.

## Oak Bluffs

Oak Bluffs Town Beach is a calm, shallow beach with fine sand that runs from the harbor entrance, an area called Inkwell Beach, all the way past the Steamship Authority's piers to State Beach. It is open to all.

Eastville Beach is located just over the bridge dividing Vineyard Haven and Oak Bluffs. It is a public beach open to all.

## Vineyard Haven

Owen Park Beach, Vineyard Haven's public beach, is on the harbor just a short distance (heading toward West Chop) from the Steamship Authority piers and offices. It runs from the ferry dock on the harbor to the town dock at Owen Park.

Lake Tashmoo is outside of Vineyard Haven on the north shore. To reach it, you can go out Main Street or Franklin Street, heading toward West Chop. Turn left on Daggett Avenue and follow it to Herring Creek Road, a dirt road that goes down to the beach. The beach is sandy, there is usually a fair current at the entrance to Vineyard Sound, and it is open to all.

*Digging in the sand at State Beach, where the sea is gentle.*

## West Tisbury

Long Point Wildlife Refuge is located along the Atlantic Ocean and Tisbury Great Pond. It is a 580-acre preserve managed by the Trustees of Reservations. They own a half mile of South Beach, and swimming, surf fishing, and picnicking are permitted here. They also offer wildlife and history tours in their kayaks and canoes. There is an admission fee of $3.00 per person ages fifteen and older and a charge of $10.00 per vehicle. There is also a limit of fifty-five cars per day. To reach Long Point, take Waldron's Bottom Road, which is exactly 1 mile west of the entrance to Martha's Vineyard Airport, and follow the signs along this narrow, bumpy dirt road for 3 miles to the refuge. It is open to all. Behind the ocean beach is the quiet Tisbury Great Pond, which is also enjoyable.

Lambert's Cove Beach is on the north shore in West Tisbury. Unlike many areas along the north shore where the beach is pebbly, here there is fine sand. The beach is only for West Tisbury residents, their guests, and any guests at the town's inns. There is a small fee.

## Chilmark and Menemsha

Lucy Vincent Beach is on the south shore facing the Atlantic Ocean. There is a lifeguard on duty, but the beach is open to Chilmark residents, their houseguests, and inn guests only. Beach passes can be obtained for a small fee.

Squibnocket Beach on the south shore is a sandy, beautiful beach with long, slow rollers coming ashore. Some years, depending on the winter storms, it can be rocky. It is open to Chilmark residents and guests only.

Menemsha Town Beach is right beside the stone jetty at the entrance to the harbor. It is a slightly pebbly beach that's open to all, and the water is gentle and calm. There is a lifeguard here and restrooms.

## Aquinnah

Aquinnah Beach is that long stretch of ocean beach you can see from the Gay Head Cliffs, and the road running alongside the beach is called Moshup's Trail. Parking for the beach is $15 per day. It is open to the public and carefully supervised. Trespassing on the cliffs or taking the clay is against the law.

Lobsterville Beach is along the north shore of the Island. Because it is a Vineyard Sound beach, the waters are gentle and the beach is pebbly. All along the road opposite the beach, the low, rolling dunes are a protected tern- and gull-nesting area. A road here also leads over to Menemsha Pond Beach. This is a public beach, without lifeguard or facilities. No parking on Lobsterville Road.

There is no swimming or trespassing on the Gay Head Cliffs or the beach, which is a historic landmark. Moshup Trail Beach is open to the public until you reach Philbin Beach, which is open to Aquinnah residents only. Watch for signs.

# Bicycling

The Island is noted for its varied, undulating terrain. There are, however, a few flat spots for easy pedaling. They are the road from Vineyard Haven to Oak Bluffs and on to Edgartown; a short stretch in mid-Island by the airport; and State Road between North Tisbury and Vineyard Haven. The fun of riding around has been greatly improved by the addition of bike paths, which are also safer. Biking through the pines alongside the state forest, out of danger from passing cars, is delightful. (See the bicycle mileage chart and safety tips in chapter 5.)

# Bird-watching

There are many places to go bird-watching on the Island. Various groups sponsor bird and nature walks. The Wakeman Center (508–693–7233) and the Felix Neck Wildlife Sanctuary (508–627–4850) have information about other groups on the Island that also sponsor walks throughout the year.

# Boat Rentals, Charters, and Water Sports

### Edgartown

Several old wooden schooners offer full- or half-day sails and are available for private groups. There is also a catamaran that goes for afternoon sails.

## Oak Bluffs

Check local listings for information on parasailing, windsurfing, jet-skiing, waterskiing, wake-boarding, and snorkeling.

## Vineyard Haven

There are many boating options in Vineyard Haven, the home port of an extraordinary number of gaff-rigged wooden vessels; some are new, and some are very old. These sailboats take passengers for full- and half-day sails, as well as weekly charters. The Coastwise Packet Company (508–693–1699; www.coastwisepacket.com) has the topsail schooner *Shenandoah* and the pilot schooner *Alabama* for weeklong cruises for children, during which the children participate in sailing the vessels, as well as adult cruises.

*Kiteboarding at Sengekontacket Pond near State Beach.*

The famous wooden-boat builders Gannon & Benjamin have two boats for charter. Small-boat rentals are also available.

Various places offer parasailiing, jet-skiing, waterskiing, wake-boarding, and snorkeling. Wind's Up on Beach Road has sailboards, catamarans, and Sunfish. Instruction is also available. Call (508) 693–4252 or visit www.windsupmv.com. Skyhigh Kiteboarding offers lessons and tours of Martha's Vineyard. Call (508) 259–2728 or visit www.skyhighkite.com.

It's best to check the phone book for further information.

# Boat Ramps

For those who have a small boat, it's helpful to know where you can launch it. All the launching ramps are in protected bays and lagoons, but these protected waters lead out to sea for those who want to go offshore for sailing or fishing.

Boat ramps can be found at the following locations:

### Edgartown

Anthier's Landing into Sengekontacket Pond; or Katama, at the south end of Katama Bay Road, into Katama Bay.

### Vineyard Haven

Beach Road, on the Vineyard Haven side of the lagoon drawbridge, into the lagoon; or Lake Street into Lake Tashmoo.

### Oak Bluffs

East Chop Drive, along the north side of Oak Bluffs Harbor, into the harbor; or Medeiros Cove, on the west side of Oak Bluffs, into the lagoon.

### Aquinnah

At the Aquinnah-Chilmark town line at Hariph's Creek Bridge, into Nashaquitsa Pond; or Lobsterville, across the creek from Menemsha Harbor, into Menemsha Pond.

## Canoeing, Rowing, and Kayaking

The increasingly popular Oar and Paddle Association sponsors trips along the north shore, instruction, and a regatta. Kayaking and canoeing are very popular on the Island. Check the phone book or chamber of commerce for rental information.

## Children's Activities

There are about twenty-five different camps for children, and it's best to check with the chamber of commerce (www.mvy.com) or watch for newspaper notices for more information. All towns have playgrounds adjacent to schools. Other activities include:

Art, dance, language, and music instruction; check with the chamber of commerce.

Crafts, theater, and photography instruction.

Playground at the Boys and Girls Club in Edgartown.

Miniature golf in Vineyard Haven and Oak Bluffs.

Sailing instruction at Sail Martha's Vineyard and Chilmark Community Center.

Tennis clinics available in many towns, as well as at the Farm Neck Golf Club, the tennis center at the airport, and the Island Inn, including private lessons.

Junior golf program available at Mink Meadows Golf Club.

Several gymnastics day camps.

Summer basketball program in Oak Bluffs.

Figure-skating lessons; call the Ice Arena (508–693–1946).

Red Cross swimming instruction in Vineyard Haven, Oak Bluffs, Edgartown, and West Tisbury; check with the town halls or town information centers.

Public ice-skating daily, beginning in late July; call the Ice Arena (508–693–4438).

Children's Theatre, a division of Island Theatre Workshop.

Story hours at all libraries.

Preschool programs in all towns.

Day camps; tennis, baseball, soccer, and ice hockey camps.

Felix Neck summer camp.

Sports day camp, including sailing, swimming, and arts and crafts, at the St. Pierre Camp, Vineyard Haven.

Riding stables.

Merry-go-round in Oak Bluffs.

Nature and birding walks, canoe safaris, and landscape photography.

Tour of the lobster hatchery in Oak Bluffs, weekday mornings and midafternoons.

Strawberry and raspberry picking at the Thimble Farm off Vineyard Haven–Edgartown Road.

Special programs at the Martha's Vineyard Museum.

Many fascinating children's programs all summer long at the Felix Neck Wildlife Sanctuary for kindergarteners through tenth-graders.

World of Reptiles and Birds, off Vineyard Haven–Edgartown Road in Edgartown, owned by the former director of Felix Neck. Includes birds, snakes, and turtles.

# Concerts

There are many concerts and musical programs all summer long at the Tabernacle, the Chilmark Community Center, the Old Whaling Church, and various other locations. It's advisable to check the schedules in the newspaper each week.

# Evening Entertainment

In addition to the many plays, concerts, lectures, and films that go on nightly all summer long, there are many local and nationally known vocalists and bands. There are also popular restaurants that feature piano bars, jazz groups, and other performers: the Seafood Shanty, Atria, and the Wharf in Edgartown; and Lola's, the Duck, Offshore Ale, and Season's Pub in Oak Bluffs, which really swings in the summer. Outerland, formerly called the Hot Tin Roof, is the Island's casual, relaxed nightclub tucked away in the woods at the airport. It is an extremely popular nightspot and features musicians from off-Island as well as local entertainers. It accommodates 700 people and has performances year-round. Visit www.outerlandmv.com or call (508) 693–1137. Check the newspapers for announcements.

# Fall Foliage

Unlike the wildflowers, which should never be picked, dried grasses can be gathered in the fall without hurting the plants. The salt hay, oats, and other marsh grasses, milkweed pods, cattails, and bittersweet (which grows everywhere and is pretty but destructive) make attractive arrangements.

# Farms and Flowers

There are over forty farms on the Island, and many summer visitors ask where they can buy cut flowers, perennials, bedding plants, vegetables, shrubbery, and local produce. The following list of some farms and garden centers may be helpful:

Allen Farm, Chilmark; (508) 645–9046. A beautiful sheep farm alongside the ocean that sells mutton, wool blankets, sweaters, and other products.

*Sheep grazing at Allen Farm in Chilmark.*

Donaroma's, Edgartown; (508) 627–8366; www.donaromas.com. Fresh flowers, bedding plants, perennials, shrubbery, and trees. Open year-round.

Farmers' Market, West Tisbury center. Booths selling flowers, baked goods, vegetables, and plants. Wednesday and Saturday morning all summer.

Heather Gardens, West Tisbury; (508) 693–1467. Annuals, perennials, shrubbery. Seasonal.

Mahoney's, Edgartown; (508) 693–3511. Flower and vegetable plants, trees, and shrubs. Seasonal.

Morning Glory Farm, Edgartown; (508) 627–9003. Cut flowers and plants, fresh fruit and vegetables, baked goods, and meat from locally raised livestock. Seasonal.

Morrice Florist, Vineyard Haven; (508) 693–0392. Cut flowers and plants. Open year-round.

Vineyard Gardens, West Tisbury; (508) 693–8511. Vegetables and flowers, shrubs and trees. Open year-round.

## Green Thumb Extraordinaire

Polly Hill's twenty-acre arboretum (508-696-9538) is a unique spot to visit. For more than fifty years, she has planned, planted, propagated, and developed many cultivars. She is internationally known for her extraordinary work. The great favorites of everyone are the 40-foot-tall magnolias, with their basketball-size white flowers, which no one thought could possibly survive New England winters when she planted them. There are lectures and tours, and some of Polly's special collection is available at a nearby nursery.

# Film

There are movie theaters in Vineyard Haven, Oak Bluffs, and Edgartown. Check newspapers for local listings. Movies are also shown at the Grange in West Tisbury and the Community Center in Chilmark.

# Fishing

The tricky tides swirling around the Island will largely determine an angler's luck. As many as three different tides are said to converge at Edgartown Harbor. High tide at Aquinnah can vary as much as an hour from that inside Menemsha Pond. High tide at Cape Pogue on Chappaquiddick is eight hours different from that at Aquinnah, and the tide difference between Edgartown and Vineyard Haven is thirty minutes. The *Vineyard Gazette* prints a tide chart each week, and the Eldridge *Tide Book* is helpful in determining when to fish where. Some of the best shore-fishing spots on the Island are also some of the most popular. Bluefish, bonito, and striped bass are caught along the Chappaquiddick shore at Cape Pogue and Wasque and at Lobsterville Beach in Aquinnah. Some anglers have luck at the stone jetties at State Beach between Oak Bluffs and Edgartown and at the entrance to Menemsha Harbor. Scup is found in the inner and outer harbors everywhere, while the once plentiful flounder, which prefer the sandy shoals, have become scarce. Don't be concerned if you're a novice and bring in what's locally known as a sand shark; it is harmless and quite common. Cod, which are caught in the cool weather during spring and fall, are not ordinarily considered a game fish, but they have become increasingly popular with sport fishers.

# Fishing Offshore

Chartering a boat to go trolling offshore for blues, bluefin tuna, shark, and white marlin is very popular. The charters vary from year to year, so it's best to check. In Edgartown check with Coops, (508) 627–3909, or Larry's Tackle Shop at (508) 627–5088. In Oak Bluffs call the harbormaster, (508) 693–4355; in Vineyard Haven call (508) 696–4249; and in Menemsha check with the harbormaster at (508) 645–2846. Consult the paper for information about other sailboats and motorboats available for short sightseeing trips or longer cruises.

# Flight Instruction

Flying lessons are available at Martha's Vineyard Airport. It is best to go and inquire, as the availability of instructors varies from year to year.

# Golf

There are two public golf courses on Martha's Vineyard, and both are Down-Island: Farm Neck Golf Club, which overlooks Sengekontacket Pond, and the State Beach, which is located off County Road in Oak Bluffs. A semiprivate eighteen-hole championship course, Farm Neck has a driving range, a fully equipped pro shop with rental equipment, and buckets of balls for the driving range. For further information call (508) 693–2504 or visit www.harbor-view.com/farm_neck.shtml. The Mink Meadows Golf Club is an eighteen-hole course in West Chop just off Franklin Street. Call (508) 693–0600 or visit www.minkmeadows.com.

On State Road in Vineyard Haven, there's an eighteen-hole miniature golf course (Island Cove Miniature Golf Course, 508–693–2611) that is tastefully landscaped with waterfalls and plantings. Open spring to fall, it is wheelchair accessible for the first nine holes.

The Edgartown Golf Club and the Martha's Vineyard Golf Club are private.

*Menemsha fishing fleet in port.*

# Health Clubs

For those who want to keep up with their daily workout, there are several health clubs and gyms. They are Triangle Fitness (508–627–3393) in Edgartown; Vineyard Tennis Center, Workout, and Spa (508–696–8000) at the Airport; Vineyard Fitness Center (508–693–5533) in Vineyard Haven; and the Mansion House Health Club, Spa, and Pool (508–693–7400, 800–332–4112) in Vineyard Haven.

# Horseback Riding

Riding has become increasingly popular on the Island; many local children have their own horses, and families summering here for a good part of the season sometimes bring horses with them. Check out Pond View Farm on New Lane in West Tisbury (508–693–2949; www.pondviewfarm.com), Arrowhead Farm in West Tisbury (508–693–8831; www.arrowhead farm.net), Crow Hollow Farm in West Tisbury (508–696–4554; www.crowhollowfarm.com).

# House and Garden Tours

Volunteers started the Edgartown House and Garden Tour many years ago, with the proceeds going to the Martha's Vineyard Hospital. It has become extremely popular and is held every other summer. For dates, call the chamber of commerce (508–693–0085). East Chop, with its shingle-style houses on the bluff overlooking Vineyard Sound, and nearby Oak Bluffs, with its gingerbread houses, each hold house and garden tours in early July. Oak Bluffs also has a tour of the village's inns in early June.

# Island Tours

The best way to become acquainted with the Island is to take walking tours of the three Down-Island towns and a driving tour of the rest of the Island, as described in the last four chapters of this book. There also are guided tours in buses and taxi vans that originate at the ferry landings, as well as a walking tour of Edgartown sponsored by the Martha's Vineyard Museum (www.marthasvineyardhistory.org). Taxis are also available for private tours.

# Lectures

Lectures on the Island are too numerous to list individually. All the churches, performing arts centers, and other public gathering places seem to have their share of lectures each summer. Because there are so many summer visitors in the art, academic, television, and business worlds who volunteer their services for one group or another, the lecture choices are quite unusual. It's best to check your newspaper each week for the upcoming events.

# Libraries

Each of the six towns has its own public library. They all have children's reading and storytelling programs. Summer visitors may get library cards, even if they're staying only briefly on the Island, and the cards are good for one year.

*The Cape Pogue Lighthouse,*
*Chappaquiddick.*

# Lighthouse Tours

There is a mystique about lighthouses and stories of their pasts. The lighthouse at the tip of the Gay Head Cliffs and the East Chop Lighthouse are steeped in history, and both are open during the summer for one hour before sunset and one hour after. The Edgartown Lighthouse is a prized photographic spot. The Gay Head Light is available for weddings at sunset and has become very popular. All three are maintained by the Martha's Vineyard Historical Society. The Island's other two lighthouses are West Chop and Cape Pogue.

# Museums

The island has four interesting museums to visit: the Martha's Vineyard Museum in Edgartown, the Firehouse Museum in Edgartown, the Cottage Museum in Oak Bluffs on the Campground, and the Aquinnah Cultural Center (Wampanoag Museum) in Aquinnah.

## The Martha's Vineyard Museum

On School Street and Cooke Street in Edgartown is the interesting complex of buildings that makes up the Martha's Vineyard Museum. The twelve rooms of the Thomas Cooke House are furnished with early Island artifacts, including costumes, dolls, a large collection of whaling material, and more.

The main building houses the Gale Huntington Library of History and the Francis Foster Museum. The library is the Island's major historical library and repository of documents, log books, and charts used by the Royal Navy during the Revolutionary War; genealogical materials; and thousands of old books about the history of Martha's Vineyard. The Francis Foster Museum houses scrimshaw, whaling material, ship models, maritime paintings, products of early local industries, and a display of Nancy Luce's poetry and tombstones for her pet chickens.

A boat shed contains a whaleboat, a peddler's wagon, a Button hand-pump fire engine used from 1854 to 1925 (and in the Island's Fourth of July parade), a Noman's Land boat, beautifully woven Indian eel pots, and many other items. Also on the society's property is the old Fresnel lens from the early Gay Head Lighthouse.

The museum's buildings are open Tuesday through Saturday from 10:00 A.M. to 5:00 P.M. in the summer; Tuesday through Friday from 1:00 to 4:00 P.M. and Saturday from 10:00 A.M. to 4:00 P.M. in the fall and spring; (508) 627–4441.

## Some Old Favorites

- A weekly visit to the Farmers' Market in West Tisbury

- The Saturday Flea Market at Beetlebung Corner in Chilmark

- A leisurely visit to the Martha's Vineyard Museum (and make a contribution)

- The merry-go-round early in the day when it isn't too crowded

- A morning stroll through one of the cemeteries (reminder: tracings are not allowed)

- A visit to Polly Hill Arboretum

- A visit to the new Aquinnah Cultural Center (Wampanoag Museum)

## The Firehouse Museum

The Firehouse Museum on Pease's Point Way in Edgartown is right behind the fire station. It has old leather fire buckets, hats, and Edgartown's famous antique fire engine, which is always in the Fourth of July parade.

## Cottage Museum

This antiques-filled gingerbread house on the Campground at Trinity Park in Oak Bluffs will delight anyone interested in the interiors of these tiny Carpenter Gothic houses. Open Monday through Saturday during the summer.

## Aquinnah Cultural Center

The Aquinnah Cultural Center, also known as the Wampanoag Museum, opened recently in the historic Vanderhoop Homestead near the cliffs. Artifacts and memorabilia from the tribe's past are gradually being added to the collection.

# Music and Dancing

Martha's Vineyard is well known for its singers and musical groups. The individual vocalists perform at restaurants and cafes all summer long, and some of them have their own special programs at the Old Whaling Church, Outerland, the Chilmark Community Center, and other places. They vary from Johnny Hoy and the Bluefish to Mark Lovewell's sea chanteys. Other groups provide instruction in music, theater, and dancing. Check the newspapers or the chamber of commerce for dates and locations.

In Edgartown the Seafood Shanty, Atria, the Wharf, and Outerland provide live entertainment all summer. Oak Bluffs swings in the summer, and there are musicians along the waterfront boardwalk, at Season's, Lola's, and at other restaurants. The Island's musical groups also put on summer programs. The groups include the Martha's Vineyard Chamber Music Society, Island Community Chorus, the Vineyard Haven Band, and the Vineyard Sinfonietta. There are several dance groups: Martha's Vineyard Country Dance Society; The Yard in Chilmark, which teaches dance and choreography; Martha's Vineyard Dance Theatre; and Martha's Vineyard School of Ballet.

# Nature Outings

There are fifty walking trails on the Island and many special events for those interested in outdoor activities other than summer sports and beaching. The following have become more popular with each passing year, so it's best to inquire about these and any other new activities at the Wakeman Conservation Center, (508) 693–7233.

**Menemsha Hills Walk** is Up-Island in the high Chilmark hills with spectacular views. It is sponsored by the Trustees of Reservations. **Long Point Canoe Tours,** also sponsored by the Trustees of Reservations, are guided tours on the finger lake ponds that jut in from the sea in West Tisbury. **Polly Hill Arboretum** (www.pollyhillarboretum.org) is a nationally recognized arboretum; fascinating lectures and tours of this West Tisbury property are offered all year. Open Thursday to Tuesday. Call (508) 693–9426. **Felix Neck Wildlife Sanctuary** offers a variety of programs and can be reached at (508) 627–4850. Particularly fun are Beginners Bird Watching; twilight canoe trips; Creature Feature Nature Program for children three to five; Snakes and Turtle Programs for all ages; Snorkeling and Seashore Discovery Program for all ages. **World of Reptiles and Birds Park** is Gus Ben David's mini–nature center of snakes and birds off of Edgartown–Vineyard Haven Road. Call (508) 627–5634 for hours, or visit www.reptilesandbirds.com.

# Regattas

There are several annual regattas that visitors can enjoy watching. Visiting yacht clubs compete in these events. **Oar and Paddle Regatta** is held on Sengekontacket Pond on Beach Road, and local and visiting oarsmen compete. Check with the chamber of commerce (508–693–0085) for time and date. **Edgartown Yacht Club Regatta** (www.edgartownyc.org/regatta.php) is the oldest regatta on the Island, and many yacht clubs participate in this annual event held in July. Call (508) 627–4361 for details. **Vineyard Haven Yacht Club Regatta** takes place in July and is primarily for small boats. Call (508) 693–3080. **The Twelve-Meter Regatta,** held every July, is sponsored by the Edgartown Yacht Club. The prized old America's Cup boats are beautiful to watch. Call (508) 627–4361 for details about these events. Both Menemsha and Vineyard Haven have races all summer that are open to the public, including the Holmes Hole Race and the George Moffett Race in Vineyard Haven. Various types and classes of boats can participate.

# Shell Collecting

The desire to pick up a pretty shell on the beach is irresistible to most people. The shells on the Island aren't outstanding, but there are some attractive ones, particularly the scallop shells, which are found near the drawbridge in Vineyard Haven, on the Oak Bluffs end of State Beach near the bridge and jetties, around the Edgartown Lighthouse, and on Lobsterville Beach. There are almost no shells on the south shore.

# Shellfishing

If you enjoy the Island, the best thing you can do for those who live here is *not* go shellfishing at all. It is an important part of the local economy for residents, and the inexperienced or careless visitor can damage the clam beds and kill the baby scallops very easily. There is a great effort now under way to increase the growth and development of clams, oysters, lobsters, and scallops. Abuse of shellfish beds is against the law. Recreational shellfishing is permitted, however, under the regulations of each local town. Licenses are required.

# Shopping

There are many gift shops, clothing stores, handcraft shops, and art galleries, as well as T-shirt shops and souvenir stores, on the Island. Attractive shops offer hand-knit sweaters, sport clothes, unusual gifts, and antique and locally made gold jewelry. Many shops carry the work of local craftspeople—from furniture, clothes, quilts, and pottery to lovely weathervanes—and all the shops are busy on rainy days. The Flea Market, open on Wednesday and Saturday from 9:00 A.M. to 5:00 P.M. in Chilmark, has become extremely popular.

# Sports Briefs

The following adult sports (in addition to those previously mentioned) take place at various times year-round: dart tournaments; ice-skating at the arena; ice-boating if weather permits; small-sailboat races in Menemsha Pond; golf tournaments off-season; windsurfing races; lacrosse, softball, and soccer games; nature, environmental, bird, and ecology walks year-round, sponsored by Felix Neck and the Vineyard Conservation Society; and kayaking and canoeing, which have become very popular. Check with the Wakeman Center or the chamber of commerce.

# Tennis

All the towns but Aquinnah now have public tennis courts. In Edgartown, courts are located behind the Edgartown Fire Department on Robinson Road (no telephone) and at the Martha's Vineyard Regional High School on the Edgartown–Vineyard Haven Road. The private courts on the Katama Road are rented out to the public. In Oak Bluffs the courts at the Island Inn are open to the public (508-693-6574). There are town courts available on Tuckernuck Avenue (no telephone), as well as at Farm Neck, on the County Road (508-693-9728). The two town courts in the center of Vineyard Haven on Church Street have a free clinic for children under fifteen. There are courts available at the grammar school in West Tisbury on Old County Road. Reservations must be made a day in advance, but there is no telephone, so you have to go there in person. The Chilmark Community Center at Beetlebung Corner has tennis for Chilmark residents and summer visitors staying in the town. The Vineyard Tennis Center at the airport has two good indoor courts. Call (508) 696-8000 for information.

# Various Interesting Places to Visit

The Island is full of many interesting places to visit, most of which are included in the museum section of this chapter or in the Island tour chapters that follow. In addition, you may enjoy knowing about the following:

### Vincent House

The Vincent House on Main Street in Edgartown, behind the Daniel Fisher House, is owned by the Martha's Vineyard Preservation Trust and is open to the public to demonstrate how houses of the seventeenth century were constructed. Its hours during the summer are 10:00 A.M. to noon Monday through Friday.

## Flying Horses Carousel

This Oak Bluffs carousel, one of the oldest in the nation, is a must-see for Island visitors. The handsome wooden horses are more than a century old, and the carousel has been listed on the National Register of Historic Places. It is open from 1:00 to 9:00 P.M. daily, from spring through fall.

## Chicama Vineyards

On State Road outside Vineyard Haven are the Chicama Vineyards (www.chicamavineyards.com). Chicama produces several different kinds of wines from a variety of European grapes. It is the first winery ever licensed in Massachusetts, and visitors may tour the vineyard and the winery. Grapevine wreaths, wine, and gift items are offered for sale. Tours are held from 11:00 A.M. to 5:00 P.M. Monday through Saturday.

## State Lobster Hatchery

In Oak Bluffs on Shirley Avenue, off County Road, is the state lobster hatchery. Here, in a laboratory with tanks and marine biology equipment, valuable research and experiments are being done on the living habits of lobsters. The hatchery is nationally known in the scientific community for its accomplishments in expediting the growth process of lobsters, and an attendant is on duty to explain the work being done here. The hatchery is open daily, year-round, and there is no admission charge.

# Winter Sports and Activities

Winter sports on the Island can be a great deal of fun. When there's snow on the ground, cross-country skiers hurry out to the beaches to ski. There is an ice-skating rink in Oak Bluffs on the inland road between Edgartown and Vineyard Haven. Skating lessons, hockey games, and public skating are offered. Telephone the Ice Arena at (508) 693–4438 for more information. Ice-skating is enjoyed on ponds whenever the weather is especially cold.

Unlike previous years, today there are many interesting things to do in the winter. Many performances are staged at the Old Whaling Church in Edgartown, at the Katherine Cornell Theatre in Vineyard Haven, and at the high school. You can keep busy with dance classes; bridge; book

*A winter day at Chilmark's center.*

clubs; photography and art classes; nature programs, bonsai workshops, and other activities at Polly Hill's Arboretum; road races; a large health spa and swimming pool at the Mansion House in Vineyard Haven; tennis lessons; and yoga classes.

# Winter or Summer Reading

Bookstores on the Island stock the best hardcover books and popular paperbacks for the beach. The Bunch of Grapes in Vineyard Haven is large and well stocked. The popular Book Den East in Oak Bluffs has a barn full of used and rare books. In the center of Edgartown is Edgartown Books, and Sun Porch Books is on Circuit Avenue in Oak Bluffs.

There are many nationally and internationally known writers summering or living most of the year on the Vineyard, and the stores host autograph parties for their latest work. It's best to check the newspaper notices for them. Because of the large number of authors, all stores have many book-signing parties. Bunch of Grapes also has evening lectures by local and visiting authors all year round. In 2004 it was selected the best independent bookstore in the United States.

# 10

# ANNUAL SPECIAL EVENTS

## April

*Osprey Festival at Felix Neck,* celebrating the return of the ospreys (late March or early April)

*Easter-morning sunrise service,* Gay Head Cliffs

## May

*Vineyard Playhouse Spring productions* begin, Vineyard Haven (early May)

*Tour the Vineyard Bike Race,* starts from Oak Bluffs (early May)

*Scholarship Golf Tournament,* Mink Meadows (early May)

*Spring Plant Sale,* Felix Neck Wildlife Sanctuary (late May)

*Memorial Day Parade,* Edgartown

*Memorial Day Weekend 5K Road Race* (call chamber of commerce for details)

*Annual Artisans Spring Fair,* Grange Hall (late May)

## June

*Tour of the inns in Oak Bluffs* (early June)

*Oak Bluffs Harbor Festival* (second week of June)

*A Taste of the Vineyard,* Edgartown (mid-June)

*Martha's Vineyard Catch and Release Fly Rod Tournament,* headquarters are in Oak Bluffs (late June)

# July

**East Chop House Tour** (early July)

**Edgartown's Seafood Festival,** on the waterfront
   (first week of July)

**Fourth of July parade and fireworks in Edgartown**

**Oak Bluffs annual house tour** (early July)

**Tisbury Street Fair** (second week of July)

**Edgartown Regatta** (mid-July)

**Martha's Vineyard Hospital Golf Tournament at Farm Neck** (mid-
   July)

**Portuguese Festival,** Oak Bluffs (mid-July)

**Sail Martha's Vineyard Seafood Buffet and Auction,** Tisbury Wharf
   (late July)

**Monster Shark Tournament,** Oak Bluffs (late July)

## Volunteers

Without volunteer help and fund-raisers, the Island would not be able to operate as it does today. The Possible Dreams Auction for Community Services is the biggest fund-raiser. There are others all summer long for Hospice of Martha's Vineyard, the Martha's Vineyard Preservation Trust, high school scholarships, the Vineyard Nursing Association, the Martha's Vineyard Museum, and many others. Vineyard residents, retirees, and summer visitors or residents all contribute an enormous amount of time and money to these organizations. While most Island residents contribute what they can in this seasonal resort community, wealthy summer residents are responsible for making the construction of an ice-skating rink, the restoration and preservation of the Old Whaling Church, and other buildings and projects a reality.

*Annual Midsummer Eve Experience,* dance repertoire by Chilmark dance group The Yard (late July)

*Martha's Vineyard Hospital Golf Tournament,* Farm Neck Golf Course (late July)

*Vineyard Nursing Association Annual Clambake and Auction* (late July)

# August

*Edgartown House and Garden Tour* (early August, every other year)

*Annual Sandcastle and Sculpture Contest,* South Beach (early August)

*All Island Art Show,* Oak Bluffs (first week of August)

*Illumination Night,* Oak Bluffs (early August)

*Possible Dreams Auction,* Edgartown (first week of August)

*Chilmark Road Race* (early August)

*Camp Meeting Association's Cottage Tour,* at the Campground (early August)

*Martha's Vineyard Historical Society's Art, Antiques, and Collectibles Annual Auction,* Edgartown (second week of August)

*Shark Shoot Out Fishing Tournament,* Oak Bluffs (mid-August)

*Martha's Vineyard Agricultural Society Fair and Livestock Show,* West Tisbury (mid-August)

*Oak Bluffs fireworks* (mid-August)

*Edgartown Croquet Tournament* (late August)

*Oar and Paddle,* Sengekontacket Pond (late August)

*Preparing for the horse-drawing contest at the Martha's Vineyard Agricultural Society Fair and Livestock show.*

# September

***Vineyard Artisans Festival,*** West Tisbury (Labor Day weekend)

***Tivoli Day Street Fair,*** Oak Bluffs (second week of September)

***Annual Pro-Am Bike Races,*** Oak Bluffs (second week of September)

***Farm Day,*** Agricultural Hall (mid-September)

***International Film Festival*** (mid-September)

***Martha's Vineyard Annual Striped Bass and Bluefish Derby,*** headquarters are in Edgartown (mid-September to mid-October)

***Aquinnah Wampanoag Pow Wow*** (mid-September)

***Windsurfer Challenge,*** State Beach (mid-September)

*Vineyard Nursing Association Benefit Golf Tournament,* Mink Meadows (late September)

*Harvest Festival,* Agricultural Hall (late September)

# October

*Columbus Day 5K Road Race,* Oak Bluffs

*Columbus Day Artisans Festival,* Grange Hall

*Autumn Harvest Festival,* Agricultural Hall (Columbus Day weekend)

*Halloween Happy Haunting Weekend,* Edgartown (late October)

*Red Stone dancer children at the Aquinnah Wampanoag Pow Wow.*

# November

*Martha's Vineyard Skating Club Open Competition,* Ice Arena, Oak Bluffs (mid-November)

*Vineyard Artisans Holiday Festival,* Agricultural Hall, West Tisbury (Thanksgiving weekend)

*Thanksgiving Day 5K Road Race,* Oak Bluffs

*Felix Neck Fall Festival,* Felix Neck Wildlife Sanctuary, (Thanksgiving weekend)

# December

*Tisbury's Twelve Days of Christmas* (December 1–12)

*Christmas in Edgartown Celebration* (second weekend in December)

*Craft Fair,* Victorian Inn, Edgartown (mid-December)

*Daniel Fisher House Tea and Christmas Open House,* Edgartown

*First Night Celebration,* Vineyard Haven

# 11

# ISLAND ARCHITECTURE

The history of Martha's Vineyard is reflected in its houses, both the interiors and the exteriors. There are seven different styles spanning three centuries. The periods overlap, just as they did on the mainland, but with the Islanders' natural reluctance to change, the time spans were often longer and exact dates somewhat obscure. None of the original settlers' houses remain, but the earliest houses were Cape-style and were built without the benefit of an architect. Most of them have been extensively remodeled, but the Vincent House in Edgartown has not. It is a prime example of an early Cape, and, fortunately, it is open to the public.

There are full, half, and three-quarter Capes. The full Cape has a large central chimney supporting several fireplaces and a symmetrical window placement, with two windows on either side of the front door. The windows have small, square panes, usually twelve-over-twelve. Based on a style from Devon and Cornwall in England, the one-story Cape, held down against the wind by its snug gable roof (whose eaves come down to touch the front door and windows), hugs the ground and generally faces south. The steep shed roof serves as both roof and wall, the ceilings are low, and the tiny, narrow stairs are just inside the entryway, set against the chimney.

The half Capes have the front door at one end of the house, two windows, and the chimney usually directly above the front door. The three-quarter Cape is also asymmetrical, with two windows on one side of the front door, one window on the other, and an off-center chimney.

The attic room in the Cape was used for sleeping as well as for storing onions, cranberries, smoked herring, and other food that could hang from rafters. A small cellar, often called a root cellar, served as a refrigerator. It was usually a round, brick enclosure resembling a large well, where vegetables, apples, beer, milk, and other foods were kept cold.

*The Vincent House in Edgartown, built in the seventeenth century, is a prime example of an early Cape.*

*There are very few saltbox houses on the Vineyard. This one is in West Tisbury.*

As time went on and more materials became available, two-and-a-half-story Capes were built. By the first quarter of the nineteenth century, most of these houses had added a kitchen ell across the rear of the house, which Islanders called a porch. This addition was common throughout the Massachusetts Bay Colony. Often a small room in the ell was used for a creamery. With this ell—or lean-to—across the rear of the house, it had a saltbox profile. This design became popular in New England, but there are almost no true saltboxes on the Island.

Houses built in the elegant brick Georgian style (1720–80) do not exist on the Island. The wealth came later, during the whaling era. Instead, in this period the Vineyard produced foursquare Colonial houses with modest adaptations of the Georgian style. They were often built by ships' carpenters with the help of books from England. Two separated chimneys provide a central hall plan with a wide staircase, closets by the chimneys, moldings, a paneled fireplace wall, and a kitchen ell with another chimney to accommodate an iron cookstove. The paneled front door has a row of windows at the top to let in light. On the eve of the Revolution, rectangular and elliptical fanlights over the door became popular, as did sidelights, and they were often made of colored glass. Cranberry glass was the most popular; it allowed the light in while the owner could peek out without being seen. The squared-off pillars on either side of the door are set flat against the building, and the double-hung sash windows have twelve-over-twelve windowpanes.

The brief, post-Revolutionary Federal period (1776–1840) was a time of great prosperity and burgeoning architecture on the Island. The newborn nation's carpenters and shipwrights, with the help of architects in many cases, adopted the warm, delicate detail of the Federal style, which architectural historians have called one of America's "greatest architectural achievements." These large, square, five-bay houses show a mastery of composition, restraint, and grace of detail in the balusters around the hip roof. They usually have elliptical arched fanlights and sidelights, a small projecting portico, spiral staircases, and beautifully carved mantels and moldings. Even the fences, enclosing yards of clipped boxwood and yew (instead of sprawling lilacs and roses), are masterpieces of

*The Captain's House in Edgartown is a good example of
Federal and Greek Revival architecture.*

*Greek Revival architecture was popular on the Island in the
mid-nineteenth century.*

*The Menemsha boathouse is part of the history of Island architecture.*

*A typical Victorian house in Oak Bluffs.*

*The Pink Valentine in Oak Bluffs was built during the Victorian period and is a favorite of summer visitors.*

craftwork. Modest adornments from the Federal period are found on Edgartown houses built at this time. Many Island houses are transitional, with up-and-coming Greek Revival pillars adorning the portico and the delicately carved roof rails, such as those on the Daniel Fisher House.

By 1840, Greek Revival architecture had swept up the coast from Jefferson's Virginia. This style was best suited to public buildings; however, the classical doorways with pillars and the cool aestheticism of the style appealed to New Englanders, and they adopted it. Edgartown's Methodist Church is the Island's outstanding example. To imitate the white limestone of Greek temples, these buildings were painted white, and the tradition has carried on for all the houses.

As the initial fervor for these Greek adaptations subsided, a new era in architecture, named for Queen Victoria, began to appear. The Victorian era was known for its prudishness; this exterior pretense, as evidenced by lace, frills, and skirts on furniture, also found its way into the charming lacy architecture of the period with the invention of the jigsaw and fretsaw, used for scrollwork.

It was an era that the American poet Amy Lowell called "that long set of sentimental hypocrisies known in England as Victoria"; nonetheless, it did produce the fascinating architecture that can be seen in Oak Bluffs. Tents in the Campground were hastily converted into little wooden houses, each with four rooms (a living room and bedroom downstairs and two bedrooms upstairs; the cooking was done in cook tents, and there was no plumbing). All had front porches facing the Tabernacle in the center of the lawn. The lacy, wedding-cake patterns of Carpenter Gothic, with shingles like pigeon feathers, decorated every "wooden tent" on the Campground, making it a landmark in gingerbread architecture. A few other Victorian buildings can be found in the other towns.

The late nineteenth century and early twentieth century saw the birth of the large, popular, shingle-style houses in East Chop and West Chop. Many of these "cottages" were on the bluffs overlooking the sea.

The other structures that have a unique place in the history of Island architecture are the fishermen's boathouses. Without them, the town of Menemsha, which relates so strongly to the sea, would lose its character and its visual history. These simple, practical workshops are made from white-cedar shingles weathered a silvery gray in the salt air. The lobster pots piled high outside and the rope blocks, lobster buoys, carpentry tools, potbellied stoves, and all manner of gear cluttering the interior are the link between the fisherman and his vessel tied up alongside Dutcher's Dock. The fishermen's gray-weathered homes up above the bluff and the fishing fleet give the coastal village its unique character.

# 12

# VINEYARD HAVEN TOUR

Because Vineyard Haven is the Island's commercial center and principal port of entry, we'll begin our first tour here and circle the Island in a clockwise direction.

The first white settlement here began in 1674, thirty-two years after Edgartown, and was known as Holmes Hole for two centuries. In colonial times it was customary to call a protected anchorage a "hole," while the surname attached to it was usually that of the first person to use it or the owner of the adjoining land.

Holmes Hole was a village within the township of Tisbury. In 1671, when Tisbury received its charter, it was a farming community, and the center of town was the present Up-Island village of West Tisbury. As the little port of Holmes Hole began to grow with the movement of maritime traffic through Vineyard Sound, it separated from West Tisbury, established its own post office, and changed its name to Vineyard Haven in 1871. The town later was legally named Tisbury, however, which is confusing to the newcomer, who will see both names used, although Vineyard Haven is more common.

The growth of Vineyard Haven as an important seaport along the East Coast began with the expansion of trade with the West Indies and coastal shipping. It became a refuge for coast-wise traffic, and in the nineteenth century as many as 200 vessels at a time would be in the harbor to replenish supplies, ride out a storm, or wait for a favoring tide and wind. Shipyards, sail lofts, coopers, bakers, blacksmiths, and general stores sprang up along the waterfront to provision the coastal schooners, deep-water vessels, sloops, packets, colliers, and tugs that put into the harbor. Even the men and women who were farmers profited when their "bumboats," which were floating peddler's carts, went out to meet the incoming vessels to sell everything from butter and fresh vegetables to hand-knitted socks.

# Vineyard Haven

### Points of Interest

1. OWEN PARK and OLD SCHOOLHOUSE

2. WILLIAM STREET

3. ASSOCIATION HALL

4. CAPTAIN RICHARD C. LUCE HOUSE

5. JIRAH LUCE HOUSE

6. CHAMBER OF COMMERCE

7. WEST CHOP

8. EAST CHOP

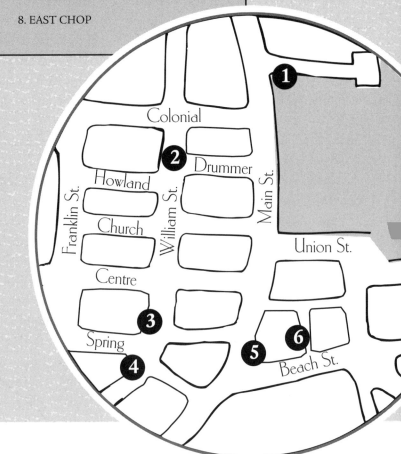

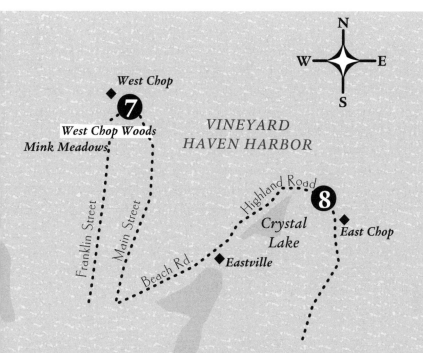

West Chop

**7**

West Chop Woods

Mink Meadows

*VINEYARD
HAVEN HARBOR*

Highland Road

**8**

*Crystal
Lake*

East Chop

Franklin Street

Main Street

Beach Rd.

Eastville

N
W E
S

Neither war nor fire has spared Vineyard Haven in its 300 years. During the American Revolution, when the British Commonwealth could no longer send troops for the Island's defense, Vineyarders maintained an uneasy neutrality. In 1778, however, Major General Gray sailed into the harbor with a large force of British troops and eighty-three vessels to replenish supplies. He called together the town authorities, explained his mission, and threatened to burn the town if they resisted. For five days the Vineyard militia was ordered to bring in 300 cattle and thousands of sheep, turn over their arms, and give up public money that belonged to the king of England.

During the War of 1812, Vineyarders were again harassed by the British. Yankee ingenuity was sorely tested in the effort to get supplies through by outwitting and outsailing the British.

## Interesting and Unusual Tours

DETAILED EDGARTOWN WALKING TOUR
Check with the Martha's Vineyard Historical Society.

GRAVEYARDS OF MARTHA'S VINEYARD BUS TOUR
Inquire at the Edgartown Information Center, Church Street.

GHOSTS, GOSSIP, AND SCANDAL WALKING TOURS
Inquire at the Edgartown Information Center on Church Street or at the Oak Bluffs or Vineyard Haven Information Centers. Inquire at the same places for regular walking tours of Edgartown, Oak Bluffs, and Vineyard Haven.

SUNSET GAY HEAD LIGHTHOUSE TOUR
Open Friday, Saturday, and Sunday.

On August 11, 1883, tragedy struck the port when a fire, which started in Crocker's Harness Shop (the present site of the Martha's Vineyard National Bank), swept through the center of town and burned sixty buildings on both sides of Main Street. Fifteen years later, in November 1898, a devastating nor'easter hit the coast, and fifty vessels in Vineyard Haven Harbor were either driven ashore or sunk at their moorings in what became known as the Portland Gale.

With the opening of the Cape Cod Canal in 1914 and the increased movement of freight along the coast by trains, trucks, and steamships, Vineyard Haven lost most of its maritime commerce. Shipping was slowly replaced by the resort business and the fishing industry; today the harbor is crowded with pleasure boats of every description as well as a small fishing fleet.

The following walking tour is a pleasant way to see the town.

# 1. Owen Park and Old Schoolhouse
## Main Street

From the ferry, walk up Union Street to Main Street and turn right. Half a block along on the right is the old stone bank, once Crocker's Harness Shop, where the great fire of 1883 started. Continue up the hill. At the crest the road to your right leads down past the William Barry Owen Park to the small public beach. There are benches, swings, and a bandstand in the park. Given to the town by Mrs. Owen in memory of her husband, whose father was one of Vineyard Haven's foremost whaling captains, it is the only public beach close to the center of town.

Diagonally across the street from the entrance to Owen Park is Nathan Mayhew's Old Schoolhouse, which has a long history. For many years it was the Daughters of the American Revolution Museum. It is now the office for Sail Martha's Vineyard and is not open to the public.

*Nathan Mayhew's Old Schoolhouse in Vineyard Haven, which now serves as the office for Sail Martha's Vineyard and is not open to the public.*

# 2. William Street

Return toward town, and just a few steps along, on your right, is Colonial Lane. Proceed up Colonial Lane 1 block to William Street, the town's handsomest street, which was spared during the great fire of 1883. It is a street of Greek Revival houses, many built by sea captains or others who had profited from the port's prosperity. These formal homes incorporated the latest improvements, such as high ceilings, a parlor heater, a cast-iron kitchen range, and a built-in sink and water pump. The exteriors, embellished with sidelights, fluted columns, and fan-shaped windows, reflected this affluence.

Bear right off Colonial at the corner of William Street for 1 block to the street's end, where you'll see the gray-shingled Grace Episcopal Church. Turn back down William Street. The houses at this end of the street were built a little later than those at the lower end; some have early Victorian details. As you continue along William Street, you will see at the corner

*A typical nineteenth-century house on historic William Street in Vineyard Haven.*

of Church Street the large, fieldstone Methodist Church that was built in 1922 after an earlier one burned. Diagonally across from the church is the Vineyard Playhouse, which presents plays in both summer and winter. It was originally a Methodist meetinghouse and became the Masonic Lodge for a century until it was converted into a theater.

## 3. Association Hall
**Spring Street**

Continue along William Street and, as you approach Spring Street, you'll see the First Baptist Church on your right. Turn right on Spring Street; the second building on your right is the Tisbury Town Hall, also called Association Hall. It was built in 1844 as a Congregational meetinghouse and was shared by the Baptists at the time. On the second floor is the Katherine Cornell Memorial Theatre, where many plays, concerts, and community activities take place year-round. The theater has handsome murals depicting the Island's history; these were done by Stan Murphy, a local artist. Funds to remodel the theater, as well as to restore the grounds and building, were donated by actress Katherine Cornell, who spent a great part of her life on the Island. The old graveyard behind the building includes Katherine Cornell's grave. She died in 1974.

## 4. Captain Richard C. Luce House
**William Street**

Return to William Street. On your right, tucked away in the middle of the block, is a large yellow house, built in 1833. It is the most elegant of the William Street homes. Captain Luce made eighteen whaling voyages before he retired, and it was his home that prompted the building of handsome and stately houses along William Street by sea captains who bought property in the area. Return to Main Street.

# 5. Jirah Luce House

Bear right on Main Street; at the corner bear left, down toward the water. A few steps away on your left is the Jirah Luce House, now a gift shop.

Built in 1804 by Jirah Luce, this is one of the few early buildings to escape the great fire that swept through the center of town. Notice the handsome doorway of this Federal house, made famous by its second owner, Rufus Spaulding. Spaulding was a typical Yankee jack-of-all-trades: physician, postmaster, justice of the peace, innkeeper, and office-holder.

# 6. Chamber of Commerce

Next to the Jirah Luce House is the chamber of commerce, where all your questions about the Island can easily be answered. This house is a typical eighteenth-century building (note the low ceilings) that also managed to escape the great fire.

# 7. West Chop

If you wish to tour the west side of Vineyard Haven Harbor, go back to Main Street and turn right. Head up Main Street past Owen Park to the West Chop Lighthouse, which is 2 miles from town.

The twin headlands of West Chop and East Chop, which cradle Vineyard Haven Harbor, protect this large anchorage from all but a northeast storm. Chop is an Old English term that describes the entrance of a harbor or channel; in the eighteenth century the harbor entrance was called "the neck." West Chop was the site of the first Methodist camp meeting on the Vineyard, in 1827.

While the architecture of the various Island communities gives them their visual character, when they began to develop as summer colonies in the late nineteenth century, newcomers had a pronounced influence on their social development. West Chop got its start as a summer colony in 1887, when many reserved Bostonians chose this area. It has, through the years, attracted retired military personnel, educators, and business-people, as well as well-known actors, journalists, television personalities, and writers. All the Island towns produced renowned mariners, and members of the Eldridge family, who once ran a ferry to Woods Hole and still publish the indispensable *Tide Book,* have long been associated with the West Chop area.

As you drive along the bluff, the houses are a mixture of very old buildings (some moved from other parts of the Island), large, turn-of-the-twentieth-century shingled houses, and some contemporary houses. The road loops around at the West Chop Lighthouse, first built in 1817, and circles around by the West Chop Tennis Club. A right turn here, onto Franklin Street, leads back to Vineyard Haven. After you make this turn, you'll pass the Mink Meadows Public Golf Course and the West Chop Woods, a wildlife sanctuary.

At the end of Franklin Street, bear left to return to the center of Vineyard Haven.

# 8. East Chop

Back in the center of town, at the five corners by the post office, take the Beach Road for Oak Bluffs. You will see a large shipyard and Lagoon Pond on your right. With sufficient warning of a nor'easter, many boats go into the Lagoon Pond to wait out the gale, just as they did more than a century ago. The lagoon is a good scalloping area, and in the winter months fishing crews can be seen raking the beds from their scallop boats. Also on your right, just before the bridge, is a ramp for launching small boats.

Just over the bridge is a peninsula of land jutting into Vineyard Haven Harbor that is a public beach and a good area for shell collecting. The small cluster of cottages along the waterfront is called Eastville, and the Martha's Vineyard Hospital is on your right. The original settlement

## East Chop Lighthouse

East Chop needed a lighthouse to warn ships away from the boulder-strewn promontory that skirts one of the busiest waterways in the country. When the government refused the Islanders' request, Captain Silas Daggett brought together a group of businesspeople in 1869 who arranged to have one built. It is one of three Island lighthouses the Vineyard Environmental Research Institute has leased from the Coast Guard, which has no funds to properly maintain them. This is also the site of the first long-distance telegraph system in the nation. A tower was erected in 1847 to relay maritime news to Boston.

here consisted of a ship's chandler, a one-room school, and several taverns. It was also reputed to be the place where mooncussers plied their trade, and it was known locally as the Barbary Coast. By hanging ships' lanterns on poles and swaying them back and forth to resemble a vessel at anchor, mooncussers lured sailing ships onto the rocks, where their wreckage was fair game for looters.

Keeping to the left and staying alongshore, bear left at the next corner onto Highland Drive. It takes you by Crystal Lake, on your right. The lake was known as Ice House Pond in the days before refrigeration, as ice was once cut and stored here. The land around the lake is now a wildlife sanctuary, but it is apt to be too marshy for easy walking.

From the top of the East Chop bluff at the lighthouse, the view across the sound to Cape Cod is spectacular. The lighthouse marks the eastern entrance to Vineyard Haven Harbor and was built in 1877 to replace an 1802 signal tower that had burned.

*East Chop Lighthouse,
built in 1877.*

East Chop was called "The Highlands" in the nineteenth century, when Baptists started their summer camp meetings here. With Methodists living in what is now the center of Oak Bluffs, going by Oak Bluffs Harbor was jokingly referred to as "going over Jordan" (one side Baptist, the other Methodist). The architecture in East Chop is a mixture of Carpenter Gothic and the large turn-of-the-twentieth-century shingle styles. Continue around a sharp curve at the bottom of the bluff; the East Chop Beach Club and Oak Bluffs Harbor are on your left.

Turn left at the end onto Lake Avenue, which leads to the traffic circle at Oak Bluffs.

# 13

# OAK BLUFFS TOUR

Founded in England in the 1770s by John Wesley, Methodism soon came to America through missionaries; its first appearance on Martha's Vineyard was in 1787, with the arrival of John Saunders, an ex-slave from Virginia. The movement quickly caught fire in America, and in 1827 the first Methodist camp meeting on the Island was held in West Chop by "Reformation" John Adams, an itinerant preacher from New Hampshire. The Revivalist service was a public forum for soul searching and emotional displays of doubt and conviction. It was a radical departure from the formality of Congregational services and attracted rich and poor alike. It wasn't until 1835 that the second meeting was held in Wesleyan Grove in Oak Bluffs. Revivalism began to sweep the Island, and preachers approached their task with extraordinary zeal as they gathered converts away from the Congregationalists. Their fervor swelled the ranks of those who came to worship in the grove of oak trees.

As the Methodist movement soared, the visitors started pitching their tents in a circle around the speaker's podium. There were family tents and communal tents with partitions down the middle to separate the sexes. In the 1870s a circus-style tent was erected in the center of the Campground for the meetings. This was replaced in 1879 by the present Tabernacle in the center of Trinity Park.

Camp meetings usually lasted about two weeks, but because many members found this seaside "watering spot" delightful, they began staying longer, and in 1864 the first of the "wooden tents" appeared. These tiny cottages, built on the tent sites, were as close together as the original tents, many not 2 feet apart. The building boom reached a feverish pitch in the 1870s when people tried to outdo each other with their Carpenter Gothic decor. The facades were gaily festooned with gables, turrets, spires, scrollwork under the eaves, tiny balconies, rococo verandas, high-pitched roofs, leaded cathedral windows, and intricately cut shingles. The owners painted their lacy valentines in vivid rainbow hues of purple, pink, sea green, blue, and yellow, making this Hansel-and-Gretel village a landmark in gingerbread architecture.

Meanwhile, more and more steamboats were advertising the delights of an Island holiday, and the town grew rapidly as a resort for secular visitors, who built cottages, shops, and hotels in the Circuit Avenue and Ocean Park area. Carpenters could scarcely keep up with the booming demands. Hordes of Methodists and vacationers poured off the boats, including cyclists in their club colors; families with trunks, bags, and croquet sets; and young men in straw hats and women in hoop skirts and bonnets.

It was a new era, and working-class people were now taking summer vacations, which were formerly the province of the wealthy. Unlike aristocratic Edgartown and commercial Vineyard Haven, Oak Bluffs was a resort and a Methodist meeting place for people from all walks of life. Huge wooden hotels, dance halls (where the song "Tivoli Girl" became a great favorite), a boardwalk, and a roller-skating rink sprang up. It became so lively that the Methodists, wishing to spare their flock the temptations brought by sinful secular visitors, built a 7-foot-high fence all around the Campground. Evidently it wasn't high enough; the holiday spirit prevailed, so they lowered the fence. Not only did the two groups mingle, but one visitor was shocked to hear the strains of "Nearer My God to Thee" wafting out from the roller-skating rink. Croquet games in the Campground reached such a feverish pitch that cheating by ministers' daughters was reported in the local paper.

To celebrate the closing of the religious meetings for the year, the Methodists held Illumination Night near the end of August. The origin of this tradition is obscure. During camp meetings, each tent was required to keep a lantern lit at night, which, an observer explained, resembled "the celestial city's pearly gates whose translucence would manifest the beauty of the glorious light within." But it was land developers from outside the Campground who first sponsored a gala Illumination in the summer of 1869 that really lit the place up. The tradition grew until Japanese lanterns hung from every tree, rail, and beam, flickering in a fairyland

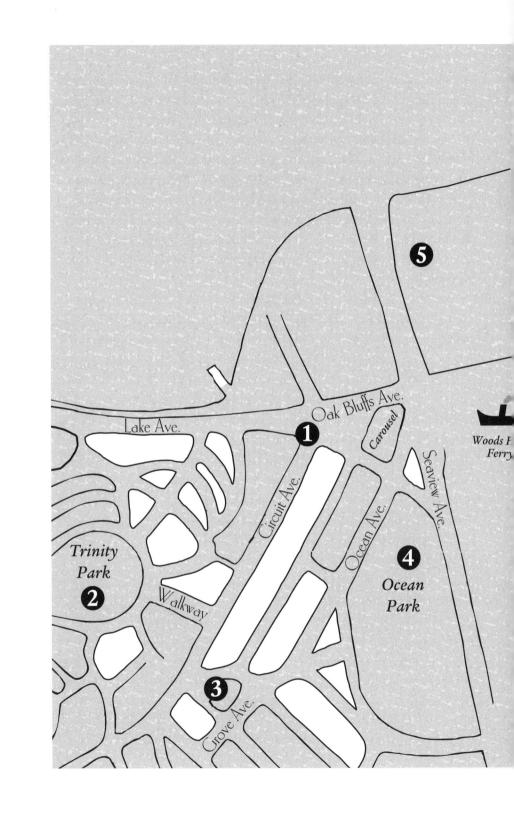

## Oak Bluffs
### Points of Interest

1. THE FLYING HORSES
2. TRINITY PARK
3. UNION CHAPEL
4. OCEAN PARK
5. BEACH AND HARBOR
6. ALONGSHORE TO EDGARTOWN

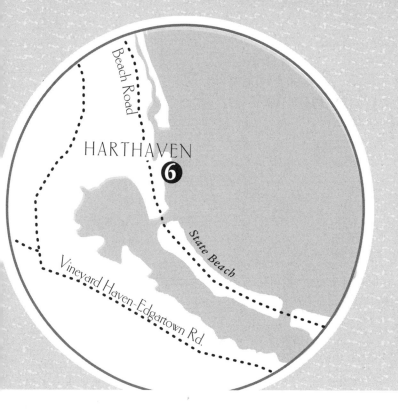

setting of tiny houses. A Japanese family who had opened a gift shop in Oak Bluffs in the 1870s influenced the decorative character of this annual event, which has continued now for more than a century.

The decline of Oak Bluffs was almost as rapid as its escalation. The hurried overbuilding (in many instances, underfinanced) the financial panic of 1873, and the burning of hotels (suspected to be arson) in the 1890s all contributed to the town's economic demise. But the Campground, while not attracting the hordes it had in the past, continued to attract the Methodists each summer in the little houses surrounding the Tabernacle. The houses are still carefully maintained, sometimes by families of the original owners who have passed them down from generation to generation. They are filled to capacity during the summer. The center of town, which is filled with restaurants, shops, many B&Bs, a few inns, movie theaters, and the Flying Horses carousel, continues to attract many vacationers, and it has grown rapidly in recent years.

You must leave your car near the traffic circle, as the only way to see this fascinating and unique town is on foot. Even bicycles are not permitted in the Campground.

# 1. The Flying Horses
### Circuit Avenue

We'll begin our walking tour at the traffic circle at the foot of Circuit Avenue, which is Oak Bluffs' main street. The Flying Horses is one of the nation's oldest carousels. The handsome wooden horses were carved in 1876 by C. W. F. Dare in New York City and were brought by steamer to Oak Bluffs in 1884. The carousel is a great rainy-day favorite for children. Concessionaires in the old building sell souvenirs and cotton candy. The carousel has been listed on the National Register of Historic Places and belongs to the Martha's Vineyard Preservation Trust.

# 2. Trinity Park

### The Campground Circuit Avenue

Take the town's main street, Circuit Avenue, which begins across from the carousel. Just before the Secret Garden, on your right, you'll see a sign and the main entrance into the Campground. Immediately in front of you, in the center of the green, is the large Tabernacle, encircled by a rainbow-colored necklace of tiny gingerbread cottages. It was erected in 1879 to replace the original meeting tent. Constructed of T-irons, angle irons, pipe, and wooden rafters supporting a corrugated roof, it is one of the largest wrought-iron structures in the United States. Like many sections of the Campground, the Tabernacle is listed on the National Register of Historic Places. Bear right here and circle the Campground in a counterclockwise direction.

The Trinity Methodist Church, the only other building inside the large grassy circle, was built in 1878. Its outstanding feature is the stained-glass cathedral windows. Walk around this fairy-tale setting of gingerbread houses in rainbow colors, each with its wedding-cake trim. Notice one with heart-shaped cutouts, others with scrollwork, cathedral windows, and little spires. They are painted lavender and white, green and orange, yellow and purple, blue and white, and any other combination that highlights the myriad forms of gingerbread. As you stroll around the circle, take time to walk a few steps down the lanes that radiate from the green; they are filled with these tiny "wooden tents."

Return to Circuit Avenue the same way you entered.

*Spring blooms in Oak Bluffs.*

# 3. Union Chapel
### Circuit Avenue

Turn right on Circuit Avenue for a few steps and go directly across the street to the Union Chapel. Built in 1871 during the heyday of the Oak Bluffs land boom, it was for those secular souls who lived outside the Campground's 7-foot fence. "When complete with the spire reaching an altitude of 96 feet," the paper reported, "it will overtop everything." This nondenominational, octagonal chapel with a domed ceiling has a balcony around five sides and eight triangular windows emerging from the rooflike spired dormers. The chapel's consecration was the highlight of a series of festive events that year: the completion of the Island's first (and only) drawbridge over the lagoon and the arrival of a new paddle-wheel steamer. The Vineyard Haven band played a new composition especially written to commemorate Tisbury's independence from West Tisbury, called "The Bartholomew Gosnold Quickstep."

# 4. Ocean Park

Behind the Union Chapel, go left on Grove Avenue to Ocean Avenue and continue along to Ocean Park. Stay on this side of the park, which is fringed with large yet dainty gingerbread cottages. A band holds evening concerts in the charming gazebo in the center of the park.

As you continue toward the waterfront, the Episcopal church is on your left, at the intersection of several roads. A Civil War monument is on the right. This statue of a Confederate soldier, painted in lifelike colors and looking like a toy soldier, was commissioned by a Southerner who had moved to the Island. It is reputed to be the only such monument erected right after the war by a member of the Confederacy. The plaque reads, THE CHASM IS CLOSED, and it is dedicated to THE UNION VETERANS OF THE CIVIL WAR AND PATRIOTIC CITIZENS OF MARTHA'S VINEYARD IN HONOR OF CONFEDERATE SOLDIERS.

# 5. Beach and Harbor

Continue past the monument to the waterfront, where the Oak Bluffs Town Beach runs along both sides of the steamship wharf. The area here and back toward the Flying Horses and the traffic circle was once the site of a huge hotel, a roller-skating rink, a dance hall called the Tivoli ("I lov it" spelled backward), and the terminus for the Island's only train, the Active, which ran from Oak Bluffs to South Beach via Edgartown for a number of years. When the hotel burned down along with the Active's turnstile, the train continued to run—forward to Edgartown and back-ward to Oak Bluffs!

Continue along the waterfront toward Oak Bluffs Harbor. You'll pass the public beach and stone jetty marking the entrance to Oak Bluffs Harbor and the pier where ferries from the Cape are docked. A short distance ahead, the street terminates at the traffic circle by the Flying Horses, where the walking tour began.

# 6. Alongshore to Edgartown

Leaving Oak Bluffs for Edgartown along Seaview Avenue, there's a small settlement of houses and an artificially created harbor on the outskirts of Oak Bluffs. Called Harthaven, it is named for the family that originally settled here, and many of the cottages are still owned by members of the Hart family.

Just beyond Harthaven is the beginning of the Joseph A. Sylvia Beach, also called State Beach, which is one of the best swimming beaches on the Island. The large body of inland water on your right is Sengekontacket Pond, a favorite spot for bird-watchers and a popular scalloping area for Vineyard fishermen in the winter months.

As you continue past the beach and enter the outskirts of Edgartown, there is a fork in the road where the inland road back to Vineyard Haven branches off.

There is a convenient parking lot here, plus bus service to the center of Edgartown and out to the ocean at South Beach. There is another public parking lot at the Edgartown Grammar School. You will want to park your car before touring Edgartown.

# 14

# EDGARTOWN TOUR

The first white settlement on Martha's Vineyard was located in Edgartown in 1642. Called Great Harbor by the early settlers, it was a self-sufficient little farming and fishing community. Lacking in trade goods and isolated from maritime traffic moving through Vineyard Sound, the village grew very slowly; it had only thirty-six houses in 1694. But with the gradual increase in Island exports and the growth of off-shore whaling, the port grew in importance until it reached its peak of prosperity in the nineteenth century.

Just before the American Revolution, Nantucket and Martha's Vineyard owned about one-quarter of America's whaling fleet. Many vessels were commandeered or sunk by the British during the war, and Edgartown's fleet suffered heavy losses. There was a thirty-year hiatus in the local whaling industry, but eventually the fleet was rebuilt, and from about 1830 until the Civil War—a time when many of Edgartown's handsome houses were built—whaling was in its prime. From Greenland to South America, from the Indian Ocean, around the Horn, to the Pacific and Bering Sea, Edgartown's ships sailed on three- and four-year voyages in pursuit of the mammals whose oil and whalebone (the latter used for women's corsets) meant instant riches.

Edgartown provisioned its own fleet and, for a time, that of Nantucket when the large, deep-draft ships needed for long voyages could not get over the sandbar at the entrance to Nantucket Harbor. Nantucket had once been the whaling capital of the world (a title later bestowed on New Bedford); Edgartown's fleet was smaller but prospered well. The wharves along the waterfront were piled high with barrels of oil where whale ships were tied up to unload or to fit out for another long voyage. A bakery turned out hardtack, one of the staples aboard ship. Sail lofts, cooperages, cordwainers, weavers, hatmakers, and a tannery were crowded together on Dock Street, along with the glowing forges of smithies. The tangy salt air was tinged with the smells of hot metal,

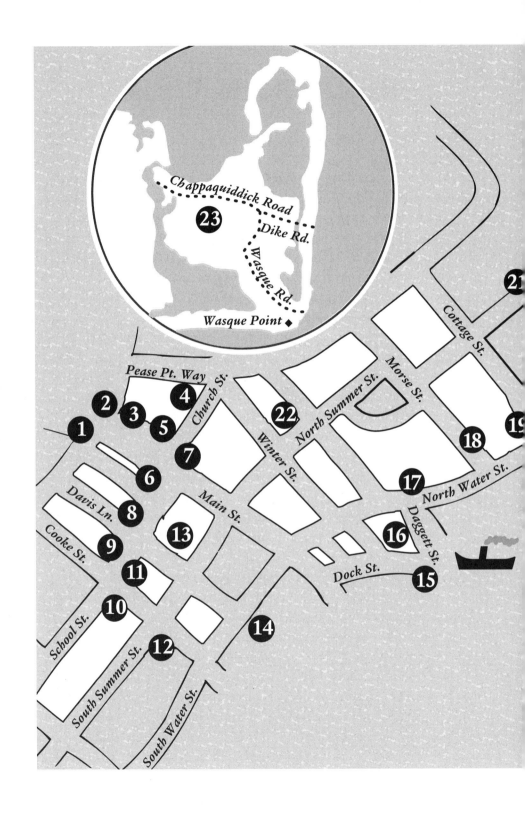

# Edgartown

### Points of Interest

1. START OF TOUR
2. CAPTAIN THOMAS MELLEN HOUSE
3. DR. DANIEL FISHER HOUSE
4. THE VINCENT HOUSE
5. THE OLD WHALING CHURCH
6. ST. ELIZABETH'S CHURCH
7. DUKES COUNTY COURTHOUSE
8. FORMER MASONIC HALL
9. THAXTER ACADEMY
10. THE MARTHA'S VINEYARD MUSEUM
11. INTERSECTION OF COOKE STREET
    AND SCHOOL STREET
12. FIRST FEDERATED CHURCH
13. THE *VINEYARD GAZETTE* OFFICE
14. PAGODA TREE
15. TOWN DOCK AND
    CHAPPAQUIDDICK FERRY
16. OLD SCULPIN ART GALLERY
17. NORTH WATER STREET
    ARCHITECTURE
18. THE JOHN O. MORSE HOUSE
19. THE CAPTAIN'S HOUSE
20. THE LIGHTHOUSE
21. EMILY POST HOUSE
22. ST. ANDREW'S EPISCOPAL CHURCH
23. CHAPPAQUIDDICK ISLAND

sperm oil, rigging tar, and hemp. Young and old were lured to the waterfront, where they hung around listening to tales of extraordinary voyages
and searched for jobs and prospects for wealth.

When the whaling era ended, Edgartown continued to have an active
fishing fleet. The town got its start as a summer resort when a hotel was
built at Katama in 1872. This venture didn't last; but just as Bostonians
discovered West Chop, New Yorkers found Edgartown and its handsome
houses very charming. Some, following Emily Post's lead, brought strict
social mores, and for generations they influenced the reserved character
of the community. New Yorkers were joined in Edgartown by people
from New Jersey and Philadelphia. Changes came slowly to Edgartown
until the 1980s, when many new inns, restaurants, snack shops, and gift
shops were introduced in the downtown area. Fortunately, 2 or 3 blocks
from the center in any direction, you will find attractive houses that
keep the town from losing its original character, and it is surprisingly
quiet, in spite of the traffic.

Edgartown has narrow streets, and the large houses are built close
together, which was common in many New England seaports where the
town was built around a harbor. The best way to see the town is to take
a walking tour, and a stroll through the town, day or night, is a delight.
It is a tradition in many New England villages to name the houses after
the original owner or, in some cases, a famous occupant. You will find
many houses on this tour referred to in that manner. There are other
fine houses not mentioned, but if you are aware of various architectural
periods, you can date the houses yourself as you stroll along.

One additional helpful note: Across Church Street from the back of
the Old Whaling Church is the Edgartown Visitors' Center. In addition to
providing valuable information, the center houses a post office and public restrooms. Shuttle buses from Vineyard Haven and Oak Bluffs termi-
nate here, as do large chartered buses from around the country.

*Edgartown's Annual Fourth of July Parade.*

# 1. Start of Tour

We will begin the tour at the intersection of Upper Main Street and Pease Point Way by the flagpole and the memorial to World War II veterans. You are a block from the center here.

# 2. Captain Thomas Mellen House
### Main Street

The gray house on your left at the corner of Pease Point Way and Main Street was the home of Captain Mellen, master of the ship *Levi Starbuck*, which was captured and burned during the Civil War. He was also captain of the *Europa*, one of the ships that rescued 224 sailors in the Bering Sea in 1871. America's whaling fleet had become trapped in the ice, and it was thought the men would die from starvation and cold long before rescue vessels could reach them. Fortunately, ships were able to get through, thus avoiding what would have been the greatest disaster in America's whaling industry. This foursquare, nineteenth-century house with a columned doorway has had the front windows changed, but those on the back wing still have the twelve-over-twelve panes. It has a central hallway plan.

# 3. Dr. Daniel Fisher House
### Main Street

The next house on your left is Dr. Fisher's handsome transitional house, built in 1840, with the Greek Revival portico and intricately carved roof rail of the Federal period. The town's most successful and versatile businessperson at the time, Dr. Fisher supplied whale oil to many U.S. lighthouses. He also owned a large spermaceti candle factory on the

*The Dr. Daniel Fisher House shows the delicate details of the Federal period and the Greek Revival portico.*

waterfront, a hardtack bakery, and the town dock. He founded the Martha's Vineyard National Bank, operated a flour mill in North Tisbury, and practiced medicine! When it came to building his house, Dr. Fisher hired a Boston architect and insisted on the finest materials. It was framed with timbers of Maine pine that had been soaked in lime for two years and was constructed entirely with brass and copper nails. From the enclosed cupola he could look far out to sea and observe the comings and goings of vessels during the height of the whaling era.

The richly carved balustrade around the roof and porch, as well as the beautiful portico, make it one of the two most elegant structures in town. It is now owned by the Martha's Vineyard Preservation Trust. The trust was formed to save, restore, and make self-sufficient any important Island buildings that might otherwise be sold for commercial purposes or radically remodeled. The Fisher house, one of six belonging to the trust, is beautifully decorated and open to the public for parties and special fund-raising events.

# 4. The Vincent House
### Church Street

On the spacious lawn behind the Fisher house is an old farmhouse also owned by the Martha's Vineyard Preservation Trust and open to the public. One of the oldest houses on the Island (circa 1675), it was moved to its present site from the Great Plain area outside of Edgartown on the south shore. It's a fine example of a one-story full Cape, with two windows on either side of the front door, a huge central chimney with three fireplaces, and tiny stairs to the attic. The steep shed roof, flush with the windows, acts as both roof and wall, and the small ell was added at a later date. The house's present windows replaced the original diamond-shaped leaded lights. The changes and additions made to the house by various owners in the course of 300 years remain.

The building exemplifies for the public how these early houses were constructed; sections of wall are left open and unfinished to show how the "wattle and daub" clay infilling was constructed. The house is open to the public in the summer.

# 5. The Old Whaling Church
### Main Street

Returning to Main Street, the building on your right at the corner is the huge Methodist church, more often called the Old Whaling Church because it was built with whaling money in 1843. The lumber was brought down from Maine by Captain John Morse in his schooner. The magnificent organ was installed in 1869, and before the clock was built, there were four handsome Gothic windows. The church is the Island's outstanding example of Greek Revival architecture. The enormous Gothic columns are its most distinctive feature, along with its 92-foot-high tower. The light in the steeple, once a beacon to sailors, can be seen by ships many miles at sea.

The church has long been an Island landmark, but a rapidly diminishing Methodist congregation put the building's future in jeopardy until it was given to the Martha's Vineyard Preservation Trust. Funds were raised for its restoration, and it is now a performing arts center. Church services are held on Sundays during the summer months only.

## 6. St. Elizabeth's Church
**Main Street**

Diagonally across the street from the Old Whaling Church is the Catholic church. Although the Portuguese had been coming to the Island from the Azores since Revolutionary times, Catholicism was not established here until much later. The first Catholic church was built in Oak Bluffs in 1880, and St. Elizabeth's was built in 1925.

## 7. Dukes County Courthouse
**Main Street**

The next building on your left is the courthouse, built in 1858 and one of the first brick buildings constructed on the Island. Originally the jailhouse was also here, but it was torn down in 1870, when the new jail and jailer's house were built farther up Main Street. All the county's business is conducted here, including sessions of the Superior Court each spring and fall.

## 8. Former Masonic Hall
**School Street**

Directly in front of the courthouse, across Main Street, take School Street. Just past the back of St. Elizabeth's Church, on your right, is a large columned building, the former Masonic Hall. It was built in 1839 as a Baptist church, but when the Baptists and Congregationalists united to form the Federated Church on South Summer Street, this building was taken over by the Masonic Lodge. It is now a private home.

# 9. Thaxter Academy
### School Street

Continue down School Street and cross Davis Lane. Notice the handsome building on your right, at the corner. It was formerly a private school and is now a private home. It was built by Leavitt Thaxter, son of the minister of the Congregational church, after he returned from sea and a teaching career in Massachusetts and Georgia. With his father's help, he built the academy. The classic form of the doorway is particularly handsome.

# 10. The Martha's Vineyard Museum
### School Street and Cooke Street

Continue down School Street, and at the corner you will see the grounds and buildings of the Martha's Vineyard Museum. This is the major historical center on the Island; it houses the Island's archives and many colonial artifacts. It has more than one hundred whaling-vessel logbooks covering the period of the Island's greatest prosperity from the whaling industry.

The Thomas Cooke House was built in 1765 for Squire Cooke, a businessman, politician, justice, and collector of customs from 1784 through 1786. It is an exceptional example of a pre–Revolutionary War house, having had almost no modifications since the 1850s.

Out on the lawn is the magnificent, enormous Fresnel lens from the old Gay Head Lighthouse. Mounted in a replica of the watch room and lantern of the 1856 lighthouse, this French lens is a national treasure. One of very few extant, it is lit every night and is operated Sunday evenings in July and August, rotating as it originally did. There is an exhibition of its history in the watch room under the lens. Behind the light is a boat shed with some fascinating exhibits. The main building houses the Francis Foster Museum and the Gale Huntington Library of History. Next door the Captain Francis Pease house has an art gallery, displays of Indian artifacts, and other exhibits. All the buildings are open to the public. (See "Museums" in chapter 9.)

## 11. Intersection of Cooke Street and School Street

The three houses opposite the entrance to the Martha's Vineyard Museum are fine examples of different types of architecture. They are all private homes.

The small farmhouse, circa 1720, is typical of many early Vineyard houses and was moved by oxen to its present location. The large, handsome Captain Thomas Cooke House, across School Street, has two end chimneys and a central hall, which was popular in the late eighteenth century. Squire Cooke built this house for himself and gave his house on the society grounds to his son at the time of his son's marriage. The small house diagonally across from the museum's entrance was built in 1820 by Captain Jethro Ripley, owner of a coasting schooner, who moved freight under sail for years. Additions have been built in recent years.

## 12. First Federated Church
### South Summer Street and Cooke Street

Proceed down Cooke Street 1 block toward the waterfront to the corner of Cooke and South Summer Street. The church here was originally built as a Congregational church in 1828, but it merged with the Baptist church a century later and became the Federated Church. It is a beautifully designed structure, and the interior contains old box pews as well as a Hook and Hastings organ. The chandelier has the original whale-oil

## Nancy Luce

Of all the museum's fascinating exhibits, those belonging to Nancy Luce are the most unusual. Luce was born in 1814 in West Tisbury. She became eccentric as she grew older. Nonetheless, she supported herself by knitting socks and mittens for whalemen and later by selling her poems to tourists. It was her adored chickens, however, that fascinated everyone. And when a favorite hen died, she had the marble carver in Edgartown make a tombstone. These stones can be seen in the shed on the museum grounds, along with the 1854 Button hand-pump fire engine and other artifacts.

*Nancy Luce was famous for her chickens and homespun poetry. Her chickens' gravestones are at the Martha's Vineyard Museum.*

lamps, and the church clock is one of the earliest bearing the name Ingraham. At night the light in the graceful and delicate steeple can be seen far out at sea. The parish house next door is an old schoolhouse that was moved here in 1850.

## 13. The *Vineyard Gazette* Office
### South Summer Street

Continue on South Summer Street toward Main Street. At the corner of Davis Lane is the main office of the nationally known, award-winning weekly newspaper that has been in existence for more than 150 years. It is located in a house built by Captain Benjamin Smith in 1764. It was at one time a home for the poor, and the four rooms, each with a fireplace, accommodated four indigent families. A large addition has been constructed on the back of the building to accommodate the growing staff of the paper, while the interior of the original structure has been carefully preserved.

*The office of the* Vineyard Gazette *is located in a pre-Revolutionary house on South Summer Street.*

Henry Beetle Hough, the late author and editor, and his wife, Elizabeth Bowie Hough, owned and published the paper for forty-eight years, until Hough sold it to James Reston of the *New York Times* in 1968. Reston's son, Richard, was the editor and publisher until recently, when Julie Welles became the editor.

Henry Hough continued writing editorials for the *Vineyard Gazette* until his death in 1984. Because of his lifelong crusade to preserve the natural beauty of the Island, Hough was known as "the conscience of Martha's Vineyard."

## 14. Pagoda Tree
### South Water Street

Follow Davis Lane 1 block toward the waterfront to South Water Street. Turn left and head back toward Main Street, but as you do, be sure to notice the fine whaling captains' houses in this area. Their doorways, roof walks, and balustrades illustrate the Colonial, Federal, Greek Revival, and Victorian styles of architecture. In the middle of the block, on the right, is the huge Pagoda Tree. The tree was brought from China in a flowerpot by Captain Thomas Milton to plant beside his new home, now part of the Harborside Inn complex. Captain Milton first put in to Edgartown Harbor while serving aboard the privateer *Yankee* in the War of 1812. He liked the town so much that he bought this house lot in 1814 and some years later built the house at a cost of $900.

## 15. Town Dock and Chappaquiddick Ferry
### Dock Street

At the corner of Main Street, turn right and head down toward the waterfront. The town parking lot and the Edgartown Yacht Club are straight ahead, but bear left along Dock Street. During the whaling era this was where the shops catering to the whaling industry were clustered together.

Ship chandlers supplied whale ships tied up at the docks, where barrels of oil for Dr. Daniel Fisher's whale-oil factory were stacked.

Dr. Fisher also owned the town dock, now called Memorial Wharf. It is the termination point of the Memorial Day parade, where schoolchildren toss flowers into the harbor in memory of Island residents who were lost at sea.

Beside the dock are the ferries to Chappaquiddick, called *On Time I, II,* and *III* because they have no time schedule other than the first and last boat of the day. The builder on the first ferry assured the town it would be ready "on time." The first ferry was actually a rowboat, and freight was floated across on a barge.

# 16. Old Sculpin Art Gallery
### Dock Street

Across from the town dock is the art gallery. This building was part of Dr. Daniel Fisher's whale-oil refinery and was later a feed mill. Its facade has not changed except for the small tower. In the early 1900s it became Manuel Swartz Roberts's boat shop, where he built catboats, which are small, gaff-rigged sailboats. They were beautifully constructed and became extremely popular. Summer visitors, Island residents, and yacht sailors frequented his shop to admire the furniture and decoys he made as well as the boats.

The gallery is open all summer and shows the work of a series of interesting artists. The interior retains its old, weathered beams and uneven, pockmarked floor. The only modern addition is the pegboard on the walls, necessary for hanging paintings.

# 17. North Water Street Architecture

Walk up Daggett Street to the end and turn right on North Water Street. The former Daggett House (now a private residence) on this corner, built

*Whaling captains' houses line North Water Street in Edgartown.*

in 1750, is the only pre-Revolutionary hip-roof house in the village. All along the street you will see some of the best examples of Colonial, Federal, and Greek Revival architecture on the Island; many of them were built by shipwrights without the benefit of architects. These independent Yankees took all the liberties they liked with the prevailing styles, and modest adaptations of the purer forms are apparent in the roof, doorway, portico, window, and chimney arrangements.

Just past the Daggett House and across the street, three Colonial houses with Georgian adornments are set at a slight angle so that the owners could see vessels rounding Cape Pogue on Chappaquiddick.

There are a number of elegant houses with handsome facades along this street. Take time to walk slowly and study their architectural details. Number 68 North Water Street, built in 1784, has one of the handsomest doorways in town.

# 18. The John O. Morse House
### Morse and North Water Streets

Just after you cross Morse Street, notice the large house on your left, the Morse House. It was built in 1840 at the height of the whaling era. Captain Morse owned a large commercial wharf down on the waterfront, just below the house, where the shipyard is now located. He was master of the whale ship *Hector,* known as "the luckiest whaleship afloat." Not only did he have "greasy luck," but he survived a battle with a sperm whale when the mammal took the captain's boat in his mouth, held it on end, and shook it to pieces. From another whaleboat, Morse buried his lance in the whale. During the height of the gold rush in 1849, he took time out from whaling to sail a group of men around the Horn to California in his bark, *Sarah.*

The original house had a porch on the first floor, looking seaward; the second-story porch was added at a later date. Some details on the facade reflect the earlier Federal period, while the heavy columns date to the Greek Revival period.

## 19. The Captain's House
### North Water Street

As you continue on North Water Street, the next house on your left vies with the Dr. Daniel Fisher House as the most magnificent Federal mansion on the Island, although they both have Greek Revival porticoes. Built in 1832 for Captain George Lawrence and sold, almost immediately, to Captain Jared Fisher, it represented the height of luxury at the time. It features Romanesque design with narrow sidelights, slender columns, gracefully carved balusters, and detailed trim on the roof walk, typical of the Federal period. Inside it has beautiful details on the ceilings, mantelpieces, and moldings.

Jared Fisher's granddaughter married into the Bliss family of Boston, and the house remained in the family for five generations before it was given to the Society for the Preservation of New England Antiquities. It is not open to the public. Notice the mannequin of a woman on the roof walk, holding a spyglass and gazing out to sea over Chappaquiddick Island. It is a reminder of the women who searched for whale ships returning from the Pacific after several years' voyage.

## 20. The Lighthouse

Continuing along North Water Street, you'll pass by Cottage Street. It was in this area that Dr. Daniel Fisher had his spermaceti candle factory.

A little farther along you come to the path leading down to the automated lighthouse at the entrance to Edgartown Harbor and the beach. Where the lighthouse now stands, there was once a lighthouse keeper's house with a light tower on top. To reach it in those days, there was a long, wooden bridge over the marshy land to the beach. It was known as the "Bridge of Sighs" because young men used to take their dates for romantic evening strolls out to the beach.

Just up the street from the path, the house on your left next to the hotel has a Dutch gambrel roof, which is very rare in Vineyard architecture.

# 21. Emily Post House
### Fuller Street

Continue past the Harborview Hotel, a beloved Martha's Vineyard land-mark. From here the road curves around the bluff and is called Starbuck Neck. The houses fronting the outer harbor are typical, large, shingle-style, turn-of-the-twentieth-century summer cottages. Starbuck Neck dead-ends at Fuller Street. Turn left here and head back toward the center of town. The fifth house on your right, past the two tennis courts, is the Emily Post House, with its beautiful garden. Considered the social arbiter of her day, Emily Post influenced the elite character of the town for years.

*The Emily Post House in Edgartown.*

## 22. Saint Andrew's Episcopal Church
### Winter and North Summer Streets

Continue straight ahead on Fuller Street to the end, turn right on Morse Street for half a block, and turn left onto North Summer Street. At the corner of Winter Street is the lovely, ivy-covered Episcopal church. The cornerstone for the church was laid in 1899, and before that, services were held in a room over a dry-goods store on Main Street.

Diagonally across the street is a fine example of an eighteenth-century half-Cape house; the dormers were a later addition. Diagonally across the street from the back of the church is one of the best examples of a Greek Revival house in Edgartown. It is now a business office.

Stay on North Summer Street until you are back on Main Street, and 2 blocks up to your right is where the tour began, at the corner of Pease Point Way.

## 23. Chappaquiddick Island

If you wish, return to the town dock, where you can take the ferry to Chappaquiddick.

It is difficult to see Chappy on foot unless you plan to take the whole day, because the main attraction is the beach on the far side of the Island, 3 miles away. When you leave the ferry, stay on the hard-surfaced road past the private Chappaquiddick Beach Club on your left, and continue up the hill. The road meanders by scrub oak, pine, and masses of grapevines; it passes a gas station, the only commercial building on the Island, and a community center for Island residents; it then comes to a sharp right-hand curve. The road straight ahead leads to the Dyke Bridge and the Cape Pogue Wildlife Refuge. On your left, just before you reach the Dyke Bridge, is the entrance to Mytoi, a fourteen-acre preserve that is well worth a visit.

Enter through the Japanese gate, from which paths lead to a bright red Japanese-style arched bridge to the tiny islet in the middle of the pond, which is home to goldfish and koi. Mytoi's winding paths are filled with wonderful flowers, trees, and flowering shrubs.

The beach here is called Wasque or East Beach and it's managed by the Trustees of Reservations, a national organization. Chartered by the state, they have been steward of the beach since 1958. Here you may fish, swim, rent a canoe, or get a ride along the beach to the Cape Pogue Lighthouse.

Return to the paved road, which goes to Wasque Point, a wildlife reservation along the beach. There are signs directing the visitor to parking areas. Standing on this point, which is the southern tip of Chappaquiddick, and facing the sea, you can see the long sand spit on your right that connects the island with the Katama end of Edgartown at South Beach. Over the years, the sea has broken through the barrier beach and separated the two islands during hurricanes or severe winter storms. In time the ocean and currents build it back up and close off the opening.

As you return to the ferry, you'll notice driveways leading to private homes. It wasn't until the middle of the eighteenth century that Chappaquiddick Island had any white settlers. Prior to that it was a Native American settlement and one of four sachemships (tribes) on Martha's Vineyard. In a native dialect Chappaquiddick meant "the Separated Island." When some of Edgartown's residents moved here, they engaged in shellfishing and raising corn, the island's principal livelihoods. Corn was exported to Maine and bartered for cedar posts to fence the cattle grazing on open land. But the majority of residents were sea captains, and in 1878 a census listed forty-two—probably the greatest number of sea captains in any community that size.

One resident, who was part owner of the island's corn gristmill, was also a patent-medicine king. Perry Davis started the manufacture of his Vegetable Pain Killer here. Its chief ingredients, however, were alcohol and opium, and it immediately became so successful that he moved his whole operation to Providence.

At one time there was a semaphore signal on Sampson's Hill, the highest point of land on the island. This was also where the Native

Americans kept a lookout for whales and where the Humane Society boat was launched into the surf to go to the aid of vessels in distress on Muskeget Shoals. Before the Coast Guard began operating, there were lookouts fringing the island at strategic points, with the Humane Society's boats ready to be launched on a moment's notice.

The Chappaquiddick Native Americans were not treated well, and they were segregated in the North Neck area on poor land. Several Edgartownians tried to help them, but their help was late in coming: Those who did survive poverty and the white settlers' diseases moved to Aquinnah or Cape Cod.

# 15

# UP-ISLAND TOUR

This Up-Island tour will take about two and a half hours, which includes stops of ten minutes or so at various places along the way.

## 1. Memorial Park

Begin at Memorial Park on Upper Main Street on the outskirts of Edgartown, where Edgartown–West Tisbury Road is clearly marked on the signs. This road was originally called the Takemmy Trail, and in the seventeenth century it led to a Native American village on the shores of Tisbury Great Pond near the ocean. The road is inland from the sea, and all the property on your left as you drive along is privately owned. About 2.5 miles out of Edgartown, on your right, is the beginning of the 4,000-acre state forest.

Four and a half miles from Edgartown, on the left, is the Place on the Wayside, a stone marker in memory of Thomas Mayhew Jr., who often preached here to the Native Americans and was lost at sea at a young age. The Native Americans placed stones on the spot in memory of young Mayhew, who was the most compassionate of all the Mayhews, and over the years added to the pile to show their appreciation and affection when they passed by. The stones have since been cemented together, and a bronze marker was erected by the Daughters of the American Revolution.

Continue past the airport and the youth hostel, on the outskirts of West Tisbury.

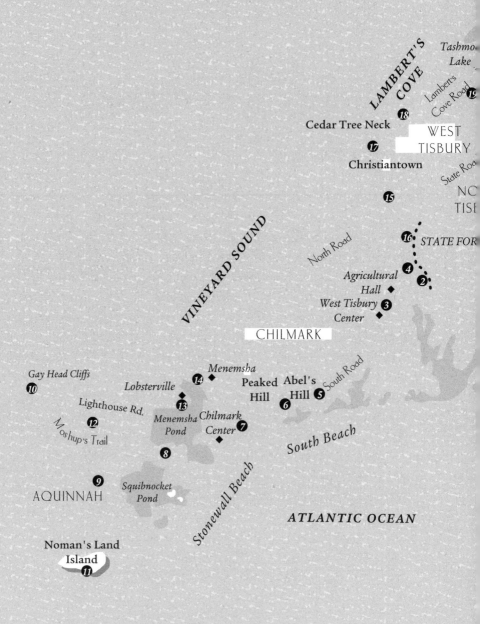

LAMBERT'S COVE

Tashmoo Lake

Lambert's Cove Road ⑲

⑱

Cedar Tree Neck

⑰

Christiantown

WEST TISBURY

State Road

NO TISE

⑮

⑯ STATE FOR

VINEYARD SOUND

North Road

④

②

Agricultural Hall ◆

West Tisbury ③
Center ◆

CHILMARK

Menemsha
⑭ ◆
Peaked Hill

Abel's Hill ⑤

South Road

Gay Head Cliffs

⑩

Lobsterville

⑬ ◆

⑥

Lighthouse Rd.

Menemsha Pond

Chilmark Center ⑦ ◆

Moshup's Trail

⑫

⑧

South Beach

⑨

Squibnocket Pond

AQUINNAH

Stonewall Beach

ATLANTIC OCEAN

Noman's Land Island

⑪

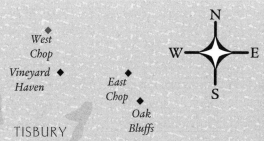

West
Chop

Vineyard ◆
Haven

East
Chop ◆

Oak
Bluffs

*'moo*
*ake* ⓴

*'od* ⓳

TISBURY

NANTUCKET
SOUND

RY
*Road*

NORTH   OAK
TISBURY   BLUFFS

FOREST   ✈ Airport

EDGARTOWN

❶ ★
START

Edgartown-W. Tisbury Road

South Beach

## 2. Mill Pond

At Mill Pond the tiny building on your right was once a grammar school and later an icehouse. The mill itself, on your left, dates back to the early part of the eighteenth century and was a factory for the manufacture of satinet, a heavy fabric made from sheep's wool that was used for whalers' pea jackets. It is now the headquarters for the Martha's Vineyard Garden Club. The pond is a fun place for children to feed the ducks and swans.

## 3. West Tisbury Center

At the T intersection ahead, the road to your right leads past the West Tisbury cemetery to North Tisbury and back toward Vineyard Haven. Bear left to continue Up-Island along the shore on South Road. A charming, rural farming village in mid-Island, West Tisbury was incorporated in 1671 and seems miles from the sea, but its boundaries cut a wide, north–south swath through the middle of the Island. Horseback riding is popular on the trails through woodlands, open fields, and alongshore. The old village store bears the advertisement "Dealers in Almost Everything." It is now owned by the Vineyard Preservation Trust. The handsome Congregational church stands on the corner of Music Street, which got its name more than a hundred years ago when every house on the street was reputed to have a piano.

Across Music Street from the church, the small mansard-roofed building, formerly the library, is now the police department, and the building on the corner is the town hall. In the nineteenth century it was a coeducational school called the Dukes County Academy and was attended by local and mainland children. Whalers also attended classes here to brush up on schooling they'd missed because they went to sea at an early age.

It is here, beside the Grange Hall, that the Farmers' Market takes place twice a week during the summer. The Grange Hall is also the site of many other summer events.

# 4. Agricultural Society Barn

Turn right on Music Street, at the church, and keep to the right (do not take Middle Road). A short distance along is Agricultural Hall, where the fair as well as other activities take place. This old barn, moved from New Hampshire and rebuilt with a great deal of volunteer help and contributions, is the pride of the Island community. The spectacular concert given by James Taylor and Carly Simon, their first appearance together in sixteen years, was the highlight of 1995's fund-raising for the barn.

# 5. Chilmark

Return to the church and bear right. A half mile beyond West Tisbury's center is the town line of Chilmark. This is a town of hills, with stone walls rolling over the moors and reaching down to the sea, clumps of scrub oak and pine sculpted close to the ground by the relentless winds, wildflowers, and windswept beaches. Old Vineyard houses as well as very modern ones dot the landscape, and the spiky Scotch broom bursts into a brilliant yellow on the moors in June. Green ribbons of marsh fringe the tidal ponds, and from the high, rolling hills, there are spectacular views of Vineyard Sound and the great sweep of the Atlantic Ocean.

Incorporated in 1694 and, like Tisbury, named for its parent town in England, Chilmark began as a fishing and farming community like other Island villages. Great flocks of sheep roamed the moors, and the placement of houses reflected a feudal system of sheep farming on communally held property. Houses were sparsely scattered over the hillsides, unlike the Down-Island towns, where they were clustered together around the waterfront.

# 6. Abel's Hill

South Road meanders along through the countryside, becoming hillier as it reaches a summit at Abel's Hill, named for a Native American whose wigwam once stood on this spot. The Chilmark cemetery has some unusual old gravestones and some famous new ones. Comedian John Belushi and author Lillian Hellman are buried here. Up behind this area is a Native American cemetery with fieldstones to mark the graves, the very small stones indicating children. While the cemetery can be visited, it is now against the law to make rubbings of these gravestones.

# 7. Chilmark Center

Two miles farther along, after passing over the little Fulling Mill Brook, which was once the site of a mill for thickening homemade woolen cloth, the road winds up a hill where open, rolling fields touch the sea. A dirt road on the left leads to Lucy Vincent Beach, which is for Chilmark residents and guests only. Just before this road, on the right, there's an old full-Cape house (number 451) with a magnificent stone wall and a place in Up-Island history.

Called Barn House, it started in 1920 as a private inn. The main house was used for meals. The chicken coops and outbuildings were converted into living quarters, and the large barn was fixed up for social gatherings. Barn House was organized by a group of extreme liberals, some of Marxist and Communist persuasion, who summered here with their families. In the ensuing years such well-known figures as Socialist Norman Thomas; Roger Baldwin, one of the founders of the American Civil Liberties Union; Felix Frankfurter, who went on to become a Supreme Court justice; and journalist Walter Lippmann visited with Barn House's founder, Stanley King, who was president of Amherst College at the time. The Vineyarders called Barn House "that hangout for radicals," although there were also more conservative vacationers in the area.

# The Deaf Community of Chilmark

In 1895 Alexander Graham Bell came to Martha's Vineyard to investigate the unusually large deaf community in Chilmark. His wife was deaf, and he was eager to learn as much as possible. But he was unable to determine why some deaf parents had hearing children, hearing parents had deaf children, or a mixture of deaf and hearing children occurred in one family. As time went on, Chilmark's insular culture (thought also to be a factor) became diversified with the rise of its resort business. Chilmark children were going off to a school for the deaf at this time, and the gene pool that had sheltered the recessive gene was gradually diluted.

The last of Chilmark's deaf inhabitants passed away long ago, but it is fitting that they have been immortalized in Thomas Hart Benton's famous painting of the deaf couple, George and Sabrina West, which is at the Whitney Museum of American Art in New York City. Benton summered on the Vineyard for over fifty years, and this was his first Regionalist painting, where, he explained, "I first turned my back on modern art." Another Benton painting of George's brother, Josie, hangs in the Martha's Vineyard Museum.

Others in the arts came here in the 1920s and 1930s, not only because they preferred Chilmark's sparsely settled, rural character, but also because it was often all they could afford. A fisherman's boathouse or a barn might be rented for the summer for $25. The informality and social gatherings, which in those days included summer and year-round residents, appealed to people in the arts.

Just before the intersection, which is the center of Chilmark, is the community center on your left, which is the gathering place for Chilmark residents. This intersection was named Beetlebung Corner for the grove of Beetlebung trees (a local term for tupelos) on your right, which are enclosed with a split-rail fence. The wood from these Oriental-looking trees, whose leaves turn a fiery red in the fall, is extremely tough, and for years it was used to make wooden mallets (beetles) and bungs to plug the bungholes of wooden casks and barrels.

*Up-Island barn.*

Chilmark Center has a former two-room schoolhouse that looks the same as it did in 1860, when it was illustrated in *Harper's* magazine. Chilmark Chocolates, which sells excellent handmade chocolate candies and butter crunch, is located next to the schoolhouse. It employs many of the Island's disabled. The town hall, firehouse, a general store, restaurant, library, and delicately spired Methodist Church complete this rural village. In 1828 this church was moved from Edgartown to Middle Road and in 1915 to its present location, where Roger Allen, a highly respected town official who was also a superb carpenter, built the steeple.

# 8. On the Road to Gay Head
(now called Aquinnah)

Three roads converge at the center of Chilmark: Middle Road, to your right, goes back to Music Street in West Tisbury; Menemsha Cross Road, straight ahead, goes to Chilmark's port; and South Road, to your left, continues on to Aquinnah.

Bear left on South Road. A mile farther along, there's a bridge, the only link to this end of the Island. There is a boat ramp on your right into Nashaquitsa Pond, and Stonewall Pond is on the left. A tenth of a mile beyond, the stone enclosure on the left is an old cattle pound that was used for stray cows and sheep when thousands roamed the moors.

The road winds up a hill to the lookout, which affords a spectacular view of Nashaquitsa and Menemsha Ponds, dotted with white sails, and hillside farmhouses weathered to a silvery gray. Beyond the ponds is Menemsha, and across Vineyard Sound the Elizabeth Islands stand out on a clear day.

The hilly road winds around the Aquinnah town line at Herring Creek. In the eighteenth and nineteenth centuries, herring was very important to the Island's economy. The fish were seined out of many Island creeks when they swam up into ponds in the spring to spawn. They were pickled in barrels for export, salted, smoked, or used for cod and lobster bait. Later the scales were sold for making "Priscilla pearls."

At the creek, the small, gray house fronting on Menemsha Pond, to your right, belonged to Missouri artist Thomas Hart Benton, who was renowned for his many murals, including one in the Truman Library. The Bentons summered on the Island for fifty-five years.

# 9. Aquinnah

Continue straight on South Road to the Gay Head Cliffs. Aquinnah is as famous for its cliffs, now a National Historic Landmark, as it is for its people. Both are deserving of their place in history. Aquinnah is one of the two Native American townships in the state of Massachusetts (Mashpee is the other). The town was incorporated in 1870, and the Native Americans were merged in the general community with all the "rights and privileges and with all the duties and liabilities of citizens."

Prior to 1870 the town was part of Chilmark. The Native Americans had always willingly shared their knowledge of fishing and planting crops, including the way to steam fish and shellfish on a beach (the origin of the clambake). In turn, the white settlers' efforts to Christianize and educate the Native Americans were well rewarded when one Aquinnah Indian went to Harvard as early as 1665, and another served in the state legislature in the nineteenth century. The Native Americans lived in loosely constructed wigwams covered with mats woven of marsh grasses. They moved from place to place, not only to let the soil rest but also to take advantage of coastal and inland climates. They lived alongshore in warmer months and moved back into the woods and valleys in winter.

The Native Americans were extremely able, courageous sailors, and because it was considered good luck to have a Native American aboard, they were in great demand as harpooners on whale ships. It was the coxswain in the longboat who cast the first iron into the whale. Native

## Writers' Retreat

By the 1920s many intellectuals and writers began spending their summers Up-Island. Many came here because the rentals were so inexpensive, while others preferred the quiet, isolated areas where they could work without interruptions. They often did find time to go Down-Island to give lectures, which were, and still are, most interesting, as noted by the local paper.

During Prohibition, Chilmark's writers and artists, as well as native Islanders, combed the beaches for bootleg liquor that had washed ashore. In no time, a wild party would be under way at the Barn House. Other times they had to settle for bathtub gin. According to artist Tom Benton, they got quite drunk on occasion.

Americans attained immortality as whalers through Tashtego, the Gay Head Indian in Herman Melville's classic, *Moby-Dick.* Another who gained local renown was Amos Smalley, the only Vineyarder known to have harpooned a white whale. Melville referred to the town Gay Head; the name was changed to Aquinnah in June 1998.

A cluster of houses alongside the main road, before you reach the cliffs, is the village center; the former one-room schoolhouse on the left is now the town library. The road beside the library leads to a beautiful Baptist church in a setting of rolling fields and gray stone walls, high over the Atlantic Ocean. Dating to the seventeenth century, it is the oldest Indian Baptist church in North America. The town's police department and town hall are across from the library on the main road.

# 10. Gay Head Cliffs, Lighthouse, and Aquinnah Cultural Center

There are ample parking areas and gift and food shops at the cliffs, which are one of the Island's great scenic attractions. Named by British sailors in the seventeenth century for their brilliant colors, the cliffs were often mentioned in logs and journals. They were a landmark to sailors outward-bound on voyages that sometimes lasted years, and for those returning to New Bedford or the Vineyard, they were the first sight of home. The twisted strata of these multicolored cliffs, which are of particular interest to geologists and paleontologists, recount millions of years of the earth's formation. Years ago Native Americans dug clay out of the cliffs, to be shipped to mainland potteries on coastal schooners. Facing west from the lookout, the Elizabeth Islands, on your right, extend in a chain from Woods Hole; the small deserted island of Noman's Land is to your left.

The lighthouse was built in 1799 after President John Adams officially approved it. It was a tended lighthouse to mark the entrance to Vineyard Sound and to warn ships away from the great reef of glacial boulders extending out from the cliffs for almost a mile. It was here on the night of January 18, 1884, that the worst shipwreck in Martha's Vineyard history occurred when the iron-hulled steamship *The City of Columbus* struck the rocks. En route from Boston to Savannah on a bright moonlit night, with heavy seas running and high winds, the vessel struck the ledge at about 3:00 A.M. It was five hours before a Humane Society boat was able to reach the vessel, where survivors clung to the icy rigging in the frigid blackness, praying and waiting for dawn. The strength of 122 passengers, one after another, gave out, and they dropped into the sea. The heroic efforts of the Islanders who rowed through mountainous waves to rescue survivors is another memorable episode in the history of Aquinnah's mariners.

*Gay Head Lighthouse, one of the Island's most popular sites, is more than 150 years old.*

The original lighthouse here was one of the first revolving ones in the country; the wooden works often became swollen in damp weather, and the keeper or his wife was obliged to turn the light by hand all night long. In 1856 this was replaced by a larger steel structure that housed a stronger light with a Fresnel lens. In 1952 the present automatic light was erected, and the old lens was given to the Martha's Vineyard Historical Society.

Just east of the Gay Head Cliffs, on a bluff overlooking the sea, is the new Aquinnah Cultural Center (also called the Wampanoag Museum). The center is housed in the Vanderhoop Homestead, formerly the home of Edwin DeVries Vanderhoop, who was a whaling captain and the only Wampanoag to serve in the Massachusetts State Legislature. The center chronicles the life of the Wampanoag tribe, which is such an important part of the Island's history. Call (508) 645–7900 for more information.

## Gay Head Lighthouse

During summer the Gay Head Lighthouse is open to the public on weekends, and the view of the surrounding sea and sunsets is spectacular. The lighthouse is a popular setting for sunset weddings. The iron spiral stairway ascends to a brownstone walkway circling the tower. The final ascent is up a steep ladder to the glass room housing the rotating beacon. There is a small admission fee.

The original Gay Head Lighthouse was built in 1799. In the nineteenth century, Vineyard Sound was one of the busiest waterways in the country. The Gay Head Lighthouse keeper counted 26,469 ships passing through Vineyard Sound in 1870.

# 11. Noman's Land Island

Standing on the cliffs, facing west, Noman's is the island on your left. Although there have been many theories, the origin of the name of Noman's Land is unknown. In the nineteenth century this was a fishing outpost for Vineyarders, who built fish houses on the north side of the island and spent half the year here, cod fishing in spring and fall and lobstering in summer. Some brought their families with them, others went back and forth to the Vineyard, and a few families lived here year-round, fishing and raising sheep. In the late 1800s as many as sixty boats worked out of Noman's Land. It is now owned by the U.S. government and will become a wildlife preserve. The islands to your right are the Elizabeth Islands.

# 12. Moshup's Trail

Facing Down-Island from the cliffs, Moshup's Trail is to your right. The road loops down along the Aquinnah beach and then connects back to South Road. The Native Americans called Gay Head *Aquinnah,* meaning "Long End" or "Point," and Moshup's Trail is named for a legendary giant and hero of both the Vineyard and Cape Cod Native Americans. Among the many stories about his extraordinary abilities is one about the boulders at Devil's Bridge, which he supposedly put down so that he could walk over to Cuttyhunk at the tip of the Elizabeth Islands. As the legend goes, he abandoned the idea before it was completed. He is also said to have dragged his toe over a barrier beach that connected Noman's Land and the Vineyard, causing the beach to disappear with the first high tide. His most famous feat, according to Indian lore, was to knock the ashes out of his pipe while fishing off Chappaquiddick, thereby making Nantucket.

# 13. Lobsterville

Again facing Down-Island from the cliffs, go left on Lighthouse Road, which makes a loop down along Vineyard Sound to Lobsterville. This was the Island's most important fishing village in the nineteenth century, before the creek leading into Menemsha Pond was dredged and riprapped in 1905 to make Menemsha Harbor. The cluster of net houses and fish houses used by lobstermen, trap fishermen, and hand-liners in the days when smacks arrived from New York to buy lobsters for 5 cents apiece is gone. It is a fine beach for swimming and fishing. (Parking is limited for both residents and nonresidents.) The Cranberry Lands across the road is a nesting site for thousands of gulls in the early spring and a favorite spot for bird-watchers. There is no trespassing allowed on these beautiful, low, rolling moors covered with wild roses, bayberry, dusty miller, and cranberries.

At the end of Lobsterville Road is a boat ramp, and just across the creek is Menemsha. To get there, retrace your steps back to Lighthouse Road and South Road, and go left back to Beetlebung Corner.

# 14. Menemsha

At the intersection, the road straight ahead is Middle Road, which goes straight back to West Tisbury. There are no historic sites on the road, but there are several wildlife sanctuaries. For this tour, bear left at the corner and take Menemsha Cross Road, which leads down to Chilmark's port, the last true fishing village on the Island. The large number of pleasure boats tied up here each summer has somewhat changed the character of the port, however.

Menemsha has its own post office in the general store, and the fishermen's colorful boathouses lining the west side of the basin have been a favorite subject of artists for years. The Island's Coast Guard station is located here, and their vessels are kept on this side of the harbor; the commercial fishing boats tie up along Dutcher's Dock on the east side of

*Lobster pots stored away at Menemsha.*

## Menemsha

Menemsha is at its best in the off-season. The storekeepers and fishermen have time to hang around Squid Row, a marvelous wooden bench on the pier where they discuss town affairs. There's even plenty of time in the late fall or very early spring for backgammon in the general store and post office.

In the 1920s, writers, college presidents, and artists such as Thomas Hart Benton and Vaclav Vytlacil were among those who found the simple, cheap rentals and primitive conditions of Chilmark and Menemsha appealing. They walked everywhere along the winding dirt roads, got their fish when the boats came in, and spent hours sunning and swimming in the ocean.

the basin. Menemsha now has a marina with plug-ins, and tourism dominates the local economy.

Menemsha Bight, just offshore, and the sea around Noman's Land have always been popular sport-fishing areas, and charter boats go out from here to the fishing grounds. The beach is open to the public.

For bikers pedaling to Aquinnah, there is a little bike ferry here. This quick crossing to the flat Lobsterville Road avoids the steep hills to Aquinnah and ends at the cliffs.

# 15. North Tisbury

Leaving Menemsha, take North Road to North Tisbury. There are no easily identifiable historic sites along this wooded, winding road, which, like South Road, is inland from the sea. The dirt driveways you see along the way lead to private houses whose occupants value their privacy and the seclusion of the north shore. There are several wildlife sanctuaries off North Road.

On the right you will pass the sign for Tea Lane, which dates back to Revolutionary times, when no true patriot would drink tea that had been taxed by England but would smuggle it in "duty-free." A Captain Robert Hillman sneaked some tea home from England for a sick relative and gave the little dirt road its name.

Several brooks along North Road run down from the Chilmark hills into Vineyard Sound. Years ago they provided sites for a paint mill, several gristmills, and a brickyard, where Vineyard clay was used to make bricks for local consumption as well as export.

Some of the Island's famous sea captains came from the north shore area, including Captain George Fred Tilton and his brother, Captain Zeb Tilton. The former gained renown for his 2,000-mile trek down the coast of Alaska to get help when America's whaling fleet was caught in the ice at Point Barrow in 1897. Zeb, a legendary coastal schooner captain who owned the *Alice S. Wentworth,* was known from Bath, Maine, to Brooklyn for his wit, skill, and attraction to women during the sixty years he moved freight under canvas.

At a fork in the road, bear left beside the magnificent oak tree with huge branches curving down to the ground. You are in the center of North Tisbury, although, increasingly, people are calling it West Tisbury, which can be a little confusing. At one time the town was an agricultural community. Here were a church, schoolhouse, blacksmith, and general store, where for years the stage from Vineyard Haven changed horses.

## 16. The Polly Hill Arboretum

Bear right at the intersection of North and South Roads; a quarter mile along is the beautiful arboretum.

It was more than forty years ago that Polly Hill and her husband began to spend the summer at a farm called Barnard's Inn in North Tisbury. An amateur gardener, she began planting all sorts of seeds, trees, shrubs, and flowers at their new summer home—magnolias and camelias thrived in this climate along with 2,000 other plants. Through the years, Polly has developed new strains of plants, which are sold in national catalogs. She is recognized internationally for her work.

Today the sixty-acre arboretum is open to the public year-round. It has a visitor center and a barn for educational and special events. Closed Wednesday. Admission is $5.00 for adults and $3.00 for children under twelve. For more information, call (508) 693–9426.

Return to the intersection by the oak tree and Humphrey's Bakery.

## 17. Christiantown

One-half mile farther along State Road, on your left, is the sign for Indian Hill Road. This leads to a crossroads and a sign pointing straight ahead down a dirt road to the Native American graveyard and chapel at Christiantown, which is half a mile farther. This ancient township was started in 1659 with a grant of 1 square mile given by Sachem Josias Keteanummin of Takemmy as a new home for Native American converts

*The Cedar Tree Neck
Wildlife Sanctuary along
the north shore.*

to Christianity. A plaque on a boulder commemorates THE SERVICES OF GOVERNOR THOMAS MAYHEW AND HIS DESCENDANT MISSIONARIES WHO HERE LABORED AMONG THE NATIVE INDIANS.

The Christiantown Meeting House, or chapel, was erected in 1829. It is a fascinating little building surrounded by a wildflower garden, and inside there is a tiny altar and six pews on either side of the aisle. The nearby fieldstones mark the old Native American gravesites.

Behind the Native American graveyard, a footpath leads through the woods to the fire-tower lookout, which commands a view of the surrounding countryside.

# 18. Cedar Tree Neck Wildlife Sanctuary

Retrace your steps to the hard-surfaced road. A right turn onto Indian Hill Road goes to the Cedar Tree Neck Wildlife Sanctuary. Several old Cape houses in this rural setting are unspoiled by development; they show what these self-sufficient Island communities looked like a century ago or more.

The road climbs to a sharp curve where a sign points the way down a narrow, bumpy dirt road for a mile to the 250-acre wildlife sanctuary. It is maintained as a "natural habitat for wildlife and as a living museum for the enjoyment of all who love the outdoors and wish to follow the marked trails through the woods and along the beach and to look out from the height of Cedar Tree Neck." With its herring pond, meadows, rocky bluffs, woodland of scrub oak and beech trees, bayberry, and freshwater stream flowing into the sea, this unusually varied terrain exemplifies the character of the Island's north shore.

# 19. Lambert's Cove

Return to State Road and bear left toward Vineyard Haven. A short distance ahead on the left is Lambert's Cove Road. Inland from the sea, with woods and hills to preclude any view of the water, it is a pretty drive through the countryside, but there are few historic sites visible from the road. Lambert's Cove was once a sizable fishing and farming community with its own ferry running to Woods Hole. A short distance in from the highway on the right is Uncle Seth's Pond, now a favorite place for ice-skating. Farther along you'll pass the Methodist church, which originated in 1846, and its lovely old hillside cemetery. Alongshore in this area there was once a brick works that produced both red and yellow brick from Island clay.

# 20. Tashmoo Lookout

Lambert's Cove Road dead-ends back on State Road by the lovely Tashmoo Farm, with its magnificent stone walls and rolling pastures. Bear left, and just ahead on the left is Tashmoo Lookout, which affords a lovely view across Vineyard Sound to the Elizabeth Islands. In native dialect *tashmoo* means "at the great spring." The opening to the sound was originally a creek where anglers used to seine for herring in the spring. It wasn't until the nineteenth century that the opening was dredged and riprapped to enable boats to enter what is now known as Lake Tashmoo.

A short distance ahead is the center of Vineyard Haven, the end of this tour.

# EPILOGUE

The fascination of an island resort is that it provides an escape from urban America. It also offers the seclusion, simplicity, easy point of reference, and strong identity of small-town America. On the Vineyard the magical attraction is not only the individuality of the six towns—the historic villages, the galaxy of entertainment in the Down-Island towns, and the bucolic Up-Island farms—but the variety and scope of the Island's natural beauty: the timeless lure of the restless sea framing the broad, windswept beaches; brilliant skies; thick woodlands of scrub oak and pine; freshwater ponds and streams; high, rolling hills reminiscent of Scottish moors; excellent offshore sailing; and the graceful movement of ships in and out of the harbors.

The soaring popularity of the Island has been both a blessing and a curse. The Vineyard is very fragile, after all, and the delicate balance between people and nature—so necessary for the Island to retain its character—is constantly being challenged. Overdevelopment in many areas is threatening this balance, and growth, often without planning, has been the source of endless controversy. It has jeopardized the water table, wildlife, wetlands, harbors, and shellfish industry. Most important of all, the Island risks losing its innate personality—that unique quality that offshore islands acquire over the centuries. The great interest in America's heritage has increased dramatically, especially on the Vineyard, where the thread of history winds through the Island like gossamer. Its historic roots and wildlife preserves are the Island's most valuable assets.

Fortunately, many dedicated individuals, both summer and year-round residents, have had the foresight and appreciation of history to understand the problem. They have worked long and hard to set aside wildlife areas and preserve historic buildings, aware that overdevelopment would not only damage the natural environment but also change the face of the Island in an irreversible manner.

Toward this end there are six organizations working to preserve, protect, and acquire properties to help maintain the balance. Currently 30 percent or more of the Island's landmass, including wetlands, farmland, beaches, and wildlife areas, is protected from any commercial development, and the work goes on. While the Island has been settled since the mid-1600s, it belongs to nature and to history, and its future depends on how citizens and visitors treat this beautiful, but very fragile, outpost.

# INDEX

# About the Author

Polly Burroughs, an award-winning author, has been a year-round resident of Martha's Vineyard since 1980. Prior to that she was a summer visitor for many years. She has written thirteen previous books, including Globe Pequot's *Guide to Nantucket* and *Zeb: Celebrated Schooner Captain of Martha's Vineyard*, as well as *The Great Ice Ship Bear, Thomas Hart Benton: A Portrait, Eisenstaedt: Martha's Vineyard, Martha's Vineyard Houses and Gardens*, and *Alaska: 1889*, with George B. Grinnell.

When she's not writing, Mrs. Burroughs enjoys such Island activities as tennis, swimming, and gardening.

# About the Photographer

Mike Wallo, a professional photographer for more than twenty-five years, is also the production manager of the *Vineyard Gazette*. Originally from New Jersey, he attended Rutgers University and worked for a number of New Jersey daily newspapers before joining the *Gazette* staff in 1980. He and his wife, Susan, and their daughter live in Oak Bluffs.